FIRST STEPS IN PATCHWORK

Anne Coleman

B.T. Batsford Ltd, London

Typeset by Express Typesetting Ltd
and printed in Singapore
for the publishers
B.T. Batsford Ltd
4 Fitzhardinge Street
London W1H OAH

A catalogue record for this book is available
from the British Library

ISBN 0 7134 64259

CONTENTS

ACKNOWLEDGEMENTS

I would like to thank all those who have allowed me to use their work. Wherever possible, I have named these people in the text, but I would also like to thank those who worked on this project but could not be named individually.

None of the group work would have been done without the assistance of the group leaders who have helped me so willingly during the production of this book. Therefore, I would like to thank Carolyn Ballard (Exwick Middle School), Sarah Dickinson (parent, helping at Compton C. of E. Primary School, Berks), Pat Fisher and Hilary Hollingsworth (Preston Young Textile Group), Audrey Furnace (Winchester Young Textile Group 2), Jaquie Walton and Philippa Johnson (East Kent Young Textile Group), Ann Jones (North Wales Young Textile Group), Gillian Laycock (Breckfield Junior School, Liverpool), Diane Mawby (York Young Textile Group), Anne Mullins (Manchester Young Textile Group), Elaine Osborne (Guildford Young Textile Group), Jo Peterson and Beverly Wood (Winchester Young Textile Group 1), Janet Russell (Birmingham Young Textile Group), Brenda Miller and Alison Sutton (parents helping at Bluecoat C. of E. Primary School, Wotton-under-Edge, Glos.), Blanche Towler and Barbara Thorpe (Sheffield Young Textile Group), Jan Parke (Pattingham Young Textile Group).

Thanks go to Sue Atkinson for her photography, Jill Wasey for her line illustrations, and Christine Bell for the book design.

I would also like to thank Peter Coleman, who, apart from taking photographs and slides, gave constant encouragement and support. Thank you, Samantha Stead, for being such an active and helpful editor.

For more information about The Young Textile Group of the Embroiderers' Guild, and The Embroiderers' Guild send a SAE to: The Embroiderers' Guild, Apartment 41, Hampton Court Palace, East Molesey, Surrey, KT9 8AU.

The Quilters' Guild is at P.O. Box 66, Dean Clough, Halifax HX3 5A.

INTRODUCTION

A patchwork is a pattern of interlocking fabric shapes. People use up pieces of beautiful or unworn fabric in this way in almost every country in the world. It would be much easier and quicker just to sew large pieces of fabric together in any old fashion, but people carefully cut and sew together contrasting pieces so that they make an interesting pattern.

American patchwork quilts are world-famous, and nomadic tribes in the Middle East use patchwork to line their tents. In India, small pieces of embroidery are sewn together in a patchwork to make a rich wall-hanging while in the British Isles people use patchwork to make cushions and waistcoats as well as large hangings and quilts. Look for examples of patchwork from America, India and the Middle East and notice the similarities and the differences.

People in all these countries like to take a little more time and make something which looks exciting and beautiful, as well as being useful. Patchwork patterns are formed by the colour, tone and shape of the fabric pieces used. Dark-toned patches may be placed next to light tones to make a contrast, or the patches might be placed so that dark patches gradually shade to light patches.

Some geometric shapes interlock to cover an area without leaving spaces, and these are often used in patchwork. Other geometric shapes need only one other shape to fill in the spaces. Any picture can

Window and brick patterns. Chester.

be divided up with straight lines into smaller shapes to make a patchwork.

Fabric is not the only material where small pieces are put together to make a larger pattern. Look at a mosaic floor, or the coloured wall and floor tiles in a bathroom or a kitchen, or even paving stones and cobbles. A stained-glass window is only a collection of different coloured interlocking glass pieces.

In aerial pictures or in hilly country, fields appear to fit together to make a patchwork. Notice how the different colours, tones and shapes make an all-over pattern.

Traditionally, patchwork was sewn because the fabric formed was used to make things to wear and use and had therefore to be hard-wearing. However patchwork patterns used for decoration only do not need to be strong so the fabric shapes, once arranged in patterns, may just as well be stuck in place. Hand-sewn patchwork can be used for smaller pieces of work, while large pieces of patchwork can be joined much more quickly on a sewing machine.

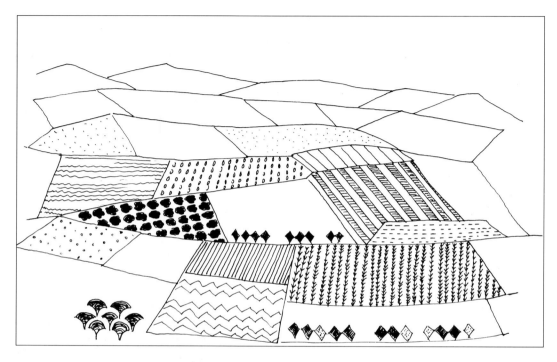

Landscape in Provence.

MATERIALS FOR PATCHWORK

The fabric

There are many different types of fabric. A visit to the fabric department of a store will show you that the choice is enormous. And of course soft furnishings, carpets, rugs, tents, and parachutes are all made of fabric as well as clothes. The fabrics you need for patchwork can be bought new, adapted to your requirements by printing or dyeing, or recycled from unworn parts of old garments.

Fibre types

Most fabrics are made from yarns. Yarns are made from fibres which can be divided into groups:
a] natural fibres: these are fibres made from plants or animal coats, e.g. cotton, wool, silk;
b] man-made fibres: these fibres are made from things like wood pulp, e.g. viscose;
c] synthetic fibres: these are made from petrochemicals then spun to imitate natural yarns, e.g. polyester, nylon.

Fibres have different properties: some will not crease, some are warm, some resist dirt and some do not wear out quickly. Fibres are often mixed to make a particular fabric, for example polyester-cotton. It is some-times difficult to tell what fibres go to make up a fabric but all fabrics now have to be marked with their fibre content. Look at the labels on new rolls of fabric in a shop or on your own clothes.

Threads

In patchwork the small shapes are usually sewn together to make a large piece of fabric. Whether this is done by hand or using a machine, a smooth, firm, strong thread is required. Sewing threads are readily available from haberdashers, from large stores, from craft suppliers and often from small shops and general stores. Most are made from cotton, cotton-polyester, or all polyester. Silk thread is also available.

Choose a thread which goes with the fabric you are using, that is, cotton for all-cotton fabrics, cotton-polyester and polyester for synthetic fabrics and mixes. When in doubt, use cotton-polyester thread. These products can be used for both hand and machine sewing. Tacking cotton should be used only for tacking fabrics together before sewing as it is not strong enough for finished work.

You may eventually want to quilt your patchwork. Apart from the threads already mentioned, you might use quilting cotton, machine embroidery cotton or even coton-à-broder, two or three strands of stranded cotton or fine crochet cotton for a more decorative effect. If you think a thread will look good, and if it is strong enough, go ahead and use it.

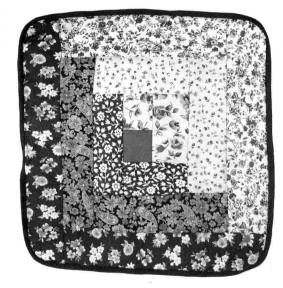

Log cabin patchwork. Gillian Brittain.

Fabric construction

All yarns or fibres are knitted, felted or woven to make fabric. This is important in patchwork because you need to choose just the right fabric for your project. The construction of a fabric gives it particular properties. Look at a variety of fabrics under a magnifier; compare the way they feel, stretch and distort, fray and tear. The sort of fabric you use depends on what you are making.

Woven fabrics

Woven fabrics will lie flat as long as the patches are cut on the straight grain of the fabric. If this is quite impossible, it may be necessary to back the fabric with iron-on interfacing. Choose a woven fabric to make anything which is to be worn and washed or cleaned. Patchwork is often made from woven cotton because this is particularly easy to handle. Also, woven cotton will often tear easily along the weave, which is very useful for strip patchwork because you will not need to use a template.

Woven silk, velvet and woven glitter fabrics, and see-through fabric such as organza are sumptuous and exciting and make lovely rich-looking patchwork. Woollen patchwork made with tweed is very hard-wearing.

Knitted fabrics

Knitted fabrics stretch easily. However, this is not a problem if you are making a picture or a pattern to display rather than to wear, or if you are sticking rather than sewing. Some of the shapes can be padded to make them stand out.

If you make a knitted patchwork to wear, *all* the shapes should be knitted, pressed and arranged before they are sewn together with back stitch or oversewing. Commercial knitted fabrics include jersey and nylon knit.

Felt fabrics

Felt fabrics tear easily but are popular for pictures, patterns and decorative items which do not need washing. Many people make their own felt and small pieces of hand-made felt can look very effective when sewn together to make a patchwork.

If you are making something to wear or use, all the patches should be made from the *same type* of fabric, for instance, silk, cotton or wool, and the fabrics should also be of the same weight or thickness.

For a picture, a wall-hanging or something which does not need to be washed or cleaned, almost any type of fabric can be used as long as it looks right. Suede, leather, plastic, lace and ribbon can all be used for patchwork.

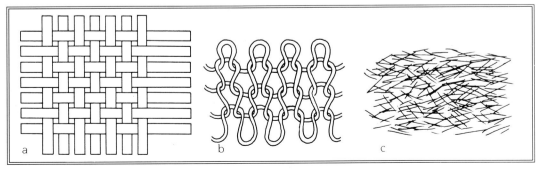

(a) Woven fabric; (b) knitted fabric; (c) felted fabric.

Colour and pattern

Fabrics can also be divided into groups according to colour and pattern. If you look at a piece of fabric, whether it is plain coloured or printed, it will have a 'tone' on a scale which ranges from very pale to very dark. It is sometimes easier to see this with half-closed eyes. Not only fabric but everything else in the environment, indeed, can be divided into tones from light to dark. If you place a pale piece of fabric next to a dark piece, it makes a contrast. Tone is particularly important in patchwork because the dark and light tones create the pattern. Always think of tone when you compare and match pieces of fabric.

Plain-coloured fabrics

Look carefully at the tones of plain-coloured fabrics ranging from dark to pale. Different textures, hairy, smooth, woolly and shiny, all make the basic colour tone look slightly different. Some fabrics have a warp which is a different colour from the weft. When seen from different angles the fabric seems to be another colour altogether. Patches cut from 'shot' fabrics can be most attractive when used together if every alternate patch is turned to exploit this effect.

Collect some tones of the same colour and range them from pale to dark.

You can also make patterns by cutting out free-hand shapes such as squares and triangles and arranging them in different ways.

Patterned fabrics

The wide range of patterned fabrics on the market is produced by different processes.

Woven

Different coloured yarns may be woven together to make a pattern, as seen in woollen tweeds, or same-coloured yarns woven together in different patterns as in damask.

(a) Tone: light to dark.
(b) Stripes rearranged.

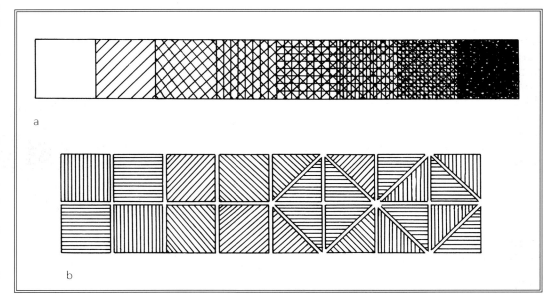

a

b

Printed

Fabrics with small even patterns: some patterns are dense while others are scattered and look almost like a texture from a distance. As with plain colours each patterned fabric has a dominant colour and tone.

Stripes: these might be wide or narrow. Patches cut from stripes can be turned to make all sorts of exciting patterns.

Large patterns: parts of these fabrics can often be utilized for patchwork. Interesting results come from choosing just the right pieces.

Look at a whole collection of fabrics and try to match some of the colours: Find a plain fabric which matches one of the colours in a patterned fabric. Find a light and a dark patterned fabric which go together. Compare the tones of fabrics printed in different colourways. A patterned fabric might be made up of three or more colours. Compare a piece of each plain colour with this fabric. Which combination do you prefer?

(c) *Fabric textures.*
(d) *Yarns woven in different colours.*
(e) *Printed patterns.*
(f) *Part of a large pattern.*

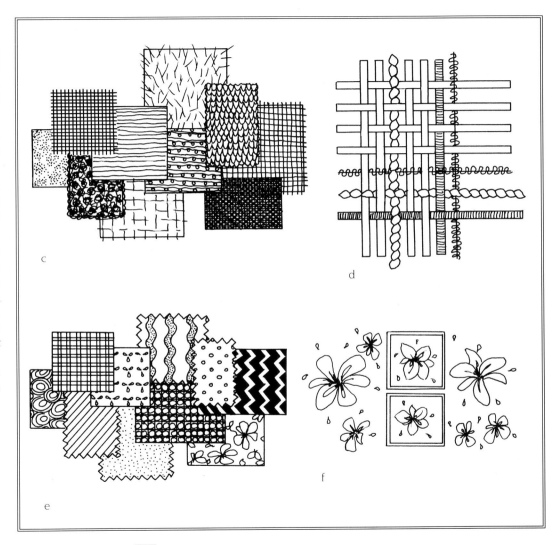

c

d

e

f

Colouring your own fabrics

Fabrics are quite expensive and you might not be able to find just what you want anyway. It is often fun to produce a unique pattern of your own. There are many ways of colouring and patterning fabrics, and all can be done at home or in a small workroom. Make sure you read the instructions on the packets, bottles or boxes of dye and paint to get a really good result.

Always colour or print your fabric before making it up into patchwork.

Dyeing

You can dye fabrics with household dyes available from the haberdashery departments of large stores or from art and craft suppliers. They are easy to use and some can even be used in a washing machine or a microwave, but you must follow the instructions carefully. Certain dyes dye particular fabrics only and one packet of dye will colour only a certain weight of fabric. You may have to add another ingredient such as salt or soda. All ingredients must be measured carefully.

Protect yourself with an overall and rubber gloves, and cover all surrounding surfaces with plastic sheeting or newspaper. Use plastic buckets, containers and measuring spoons (rather than metal) and keep spare dyes in a safe place in clearly labelled jars. Once the dyes are mixed with salt or dye-fix, use them immediately.

Soak new fabrics in detergent to get rid of the dressing before you start.

Try dyeing white or cream cotton, good parts of old sheets or calico. Coloured and patterned fabrics can also be overdyed. Notice how the dye changes the basic colour of the fabrics.

You can also dye one fabric in random colours by placing the fabric in a flat plastic container, mixing two separate cold-water dyes in two jars and gently pouring some of each colour on the fabric. Be careful not to use too much dye. Leave for an hour, then rinse.

You cannot dye a dark colour paler unless you first strip the colour with a colour remover. Hand-dyed fabrics are inclined to fade eventually but do give some lovely soft colours. They might need to be dry-cleaned in case the colours run.

Dyes are constantly updated by manufacturers so look out for new products.

Tie dye

This is a technique of patterning fabric as you dye it. The fabric is folded and tied very tightly so when it is dyed, the ties resist the colour and a pattern is formed. (See page 35) The way the fabric is folded and the position of the ties determine the pattern.

Use undyed washed cotton fabric or overdye a pale-coloured cotton fabric. It may be either damp or dry: each gives a slightly different effect. Ironing the folds in the fabric will result in a more definite pattern.

Patchwork of tie-dyed and plain fabrics.

Method

Fold the fabric diagonally or horizontally, then fold in quarters and eighths. You can also fold in a concertina, or fold all the points into the middle, or fold to make a neat little parcel. The fabric can also be crumpled up tightly, knotted or twisted.

To tie, use string, or strong fine thread such as crochet cotton or rubber bands, winding and tying tightly round parts of the fabric. Plastic-coated paper clips or pegs may be used. You can also machine or hand stitch back and forth in lines across a fabric, then gather the thread tight. Stones, buttons and marbles can all be tied into the fabric to create a variety of effects.

Dye the bundles in hot or cold water dyes or in the microwave, depending on the product you have chosen. Rinse thoroughly before untying carefully. Wash gently in detergent and warm water and dry away from sunlight.

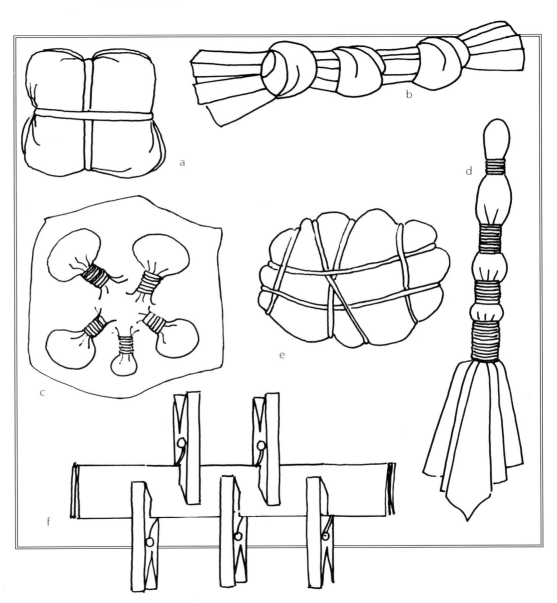

Folding and tying techniques for creating different patterns: (a) checks; (b) stripes; (c) small circles; (d) large circles; (e) random texture; (f) broken stripes.

Patterning your own fabrics

Printing, stencilling or drawing your own patterns on fabric is easy, and you can decorate your patchwork pieces in many interesting ways. Many department stores and craft suppliers, even sometimes stationers, have a selection of fabric paints and crayons which can be used at home. All paints and crayons are made fast by ironing with a hot iron for two minutes. Follow the instructions on the pack or jar. Wear an overall and protect surfaces with newspaper.

Markers

These look like felt-tip pens and are available with thick or thin points. They give clear lines and can be used to make patterns or to give a sharp edge to fabric painting.

Direct crayons

These are like pastels, and give a smudgy effect. The colours can be mixed by colouring one on another. They can also be used in conjunction with markers and plasticized paints. Iron the fabric and pin it out on a board before you begin, to get the best results from markers and crayons.

Paint in tubes

There are several types of paint which are applied straight from the tube through a nozzle, including metallic pearlized and plasticized paints. They are made for knitted fabrics but can also be used on woven

Above: Fabric markers make definite patterns.
Right: Combining different fabric paints.

fabrics for patchwork. Only the cap is removed to paint, leaving the screw-top lid in place. These paints are easier to use if the fabric is held taut and flat in an embroidery ring. Practise on a spare piece of fabric until you can get a smooth even line without blobs. The paints should be left to dry thoroughly before being ironed on the back. The plasticized paints swell up in a very satisfactory way to give a raised texture.

Direct fabric paint

Fabric paints can be obtained from the haberdashery departments of large stores or from craft suppliers to print textures and patterns on to fabric.

Below: Block prints with commercial block.
Below right: Potato printing.

Sponging

This gives a very good texture. Practise on a spare piece of cotton fabric which has been washed and ironed. You may prefer to wear rubber gloves.

Dip a piece of damp sponge into some fabric paint in a saucer and squeeze out the excess. If the paint seems too thick, dilute with water. Press the sponge lightly on to the fabric.

You can create an all-over texture or make lines and criss-crosses of sponge marks. One colour can be sponged over another as long as you allow the first to dry before applying the second. You can even sponge two colours together if you drip small amounts of different paints into the same saucer. Pressing hard or lightly makes for different textures – experiment!

Sponging.

Printing

You can make more definite patterns with a printing block. Small and effective printing blocks can be made by cutting into materials such as polystyrene, india rubber, cork, wood or vegetables such as potatoes and carrots.

Making a potato print: Use a medium-sized potato cut in half. With a pencil draw a simple shape such as a circle, a square or an L-shape on one of the cut surfaces. Use a craft knife to cut the spare potato away from the pattern so that it stands out from the cut surface.

Pour some fabric paint on to a piece of sponge in a saucer. Place a layer of newspaper on a board and cover with kitchen paper. Lay your washed and ironed cotton fabric on this. Press the cut potato on the paint-filled sponge then on to the fabric to make a pattern. Print two or three times to see which printing you prefer. You might need to thin the paint.

Potato cut-outs like this can be used to print linear and criss-cross patterns, or you can turn the potato so that every alternate print is upside down. You can also make random patterns or superimpose prints using two different cut-outs.

Stencils

This is a cut-out pattern laid on to the fabric and then painted over so that the painted pattern appears on the fabric. The most effective stencils are made up of several individual simple shapes, a stalk and two leaves for example. Use a stencil to make lines of pattern or an all-over pattern. Or combine a number of different stencils to make a picture.

Plan your pattern, then draw it on stiff

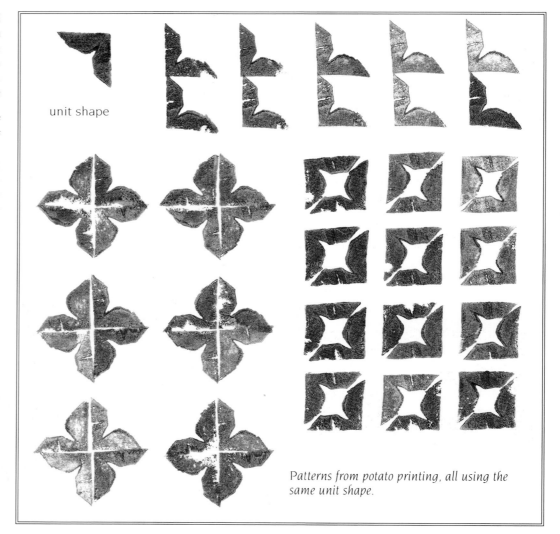

unit shape

Patterns from potato printing, all using the same unit shape.

paper, leaving a border round the edge. Use a craft knife to cut out the shapes. Place the stencil on your fabric. Press a sponge dipped in paint on to the stencil so that the paint goes through on to the fabric to make the pattern.

Stencils can also be made from sticky-backed plastic or acetate. If you want a more long-lasting stencil look for commercial stencil paper or use brown paper painted with linseed oil or shellac. Stencils may also be done using a special stencil brush or a spray. If you choose a car spray be sure to use it only in a well-ventilated room.

When you have finished painting or printing, iron the fabric carefully to fix the paint and make it permanent.

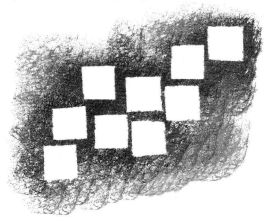

Resist using sticky-backed plastic stencils.

Cutting and using a stencil.

Silk paints

Silk paints are dyes which run through the fibres of the fabric. They can be used on any other fine, natural or synthetic fabric, but they produce particularly beautiful vibrant colours on silk. Silk habutai is a suitable fabric to use at first, but experiment with different silks. Wash the silk in mild detergent before beginning in order to remove the dressing. Dry and iron. Like other fabric paints, silk paints are made fast by ironing.

Although there is a large selection of colours, you need only buy the three primary colours, red, blue and yellow. All the other colours can be mixed. Use a saucer or a palette for this and always wash your brush before changing colour – some people keep a separate brush for each colour. Watercolour brushes of various sizes can be used for small-scale painting. Large soft brushes for painting large areas are available but you can also use a piece of cotton wool held in a clothes peg.

The silk should be held flat and taut; embroidery or machine embroidery frames will do the job well. For larger pieces of silk you may have to make your own wooden frame; bind this with strips of fabric to protect the silk. Pin the silk to the frame with dressmakers' pins, lace pins or silk pins.

Method

Many effects are possible, so it is a good idea to try them all out on a small scale. Use both wet and dry silk to see what happens. Note the difference between the results you get with each.

a] Drip the paint in two or three places and allow it to spread. Drip another colour into the middle of the first. Drip clean water into one of the drips. Notice how an edge is formed and how the colours push each other to the edge.

b] Paint a wash of colour across the fabric, then immediately apply a wash of another colour underneath so the two run together. When the paint dries, paint another pattern on it with a very thin brush, using quick strokes.

c] Drip paint on to the silk and allow it to dry. Scatter salt on it.

Notice how the salt draws the moisture into patterns. You can also dip all the silk into a solution of salt and water then drip paint on to this to produce interesting patterns.

Using resist

You can prevent the paint running freely by using a resist called gutta percha which is a type of resin. This is sold in small jars from which the gutta will have to be decanted into an applicator with a nozzle. Gutta is also sold in tubes which already have a nozzle applicator. A fine tube like a nib, which makes a very fine line, is available. This can be pushed on the nozzle.

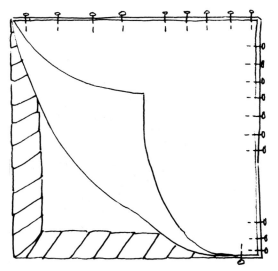

Silk pinned to a frame covered with strips of fabric.

Method

Use the nozzle to paint enclosed spaces and islands on the surface of the silk. Make sure there are no breaks in the line or the paint will run through: you can sometimes see breaks by holding the frame up to the light. Allow the gutta to dry naturally or use a hair-drier.

When the gutta is completely dry, load a paintbrush and hold it in one of the enclosed areas, allowing the paint to run to the edges. Don't apply too much paint or it will spill over the gutta line. Gradually fill in all the areas. Transparent gutta is available and also a variety of colours and metallics including gold and silver.

Allow the paint to dry, then iron for at least two minutes with the iron on a hot setting. Wash out the gutta with warm water and mild detergent.

Many variations on these techniques are possible, and by combining painting, resist, salt treatment and water, many beautiful effects can be produced.

Silk paints can also be used with batik wax, which acts both as a resist and allows the silk to be painted or printed all over without any danger of running.

(a) Gutta applicator.
(b) Gutta applicator with nib.
(c) Apply the gutta in a continuous line.
(d) When the gutta is dry, apply paint.

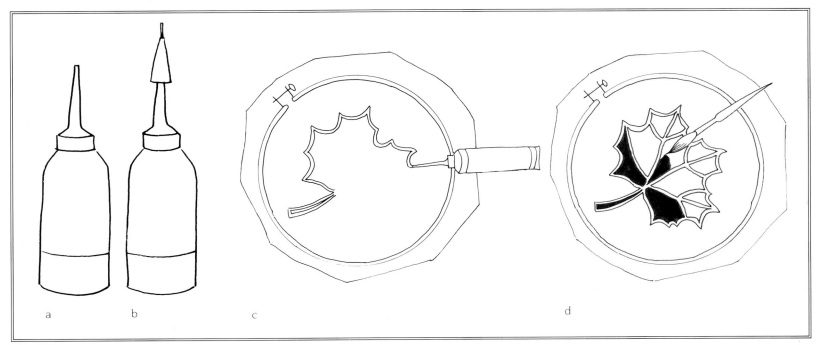

a   b   c   d

Transfer crayons and paints

These are for use with synthetic fabrics only. The design is coloured on paper, which is then placed face down on the fabric and ironed. The image appears in reverse.

Crayons

Use the crayons on paper. Greaseproof paper is best but any thin, non-absorbent paper will do.

Method

Patterns can be made in many different ways.

You can take a square piece of paper and colour it by:

a| taking rubbings of textured and patterned materials such as wood, reeded glass, wallpaper, etc.;

b| making patterns of straight lines, either vertical, horizontal, or criss-crossing;

c| colouring the paper with patches of different related colour;

d| scraping scraps of the crayon on to the paper, folding it in half, then ironing to melt the crayon. (Open out before it cools.)

The coloured squares can then be:

a| cut up and rearranged to make a pattern;

b| folded diagonally, into quarters and eighths, then cut into the edges to make a pattern;

c| printed over a stencil.

Glue the pieces down on a separate piece of paper and print. Make sure that the iron is hot enough (see crayon application instructions) and be careful not to move the paper or the pattern will smudge.

The colours should be really bright; for a more subdued effect print on pastel colours rather than white.

Transfer paints

These are quite thin like ink. Use on thin shiny paper (not greaseproof which will wrinkle with the wet).

Method

The paints can be used to paint areas of colour, to dab over stencils or to print patterns.

To make leaf prints brush the back of the leaf evenly with the paint. Place on paper, ink side down, and press to make an image. If you want to print a spray of leaves, print each leaf individually and paint in the stem with a paintbrush. Try printing with dried flowers, blocks made from vegetables, india rubber or polystyrene foam.

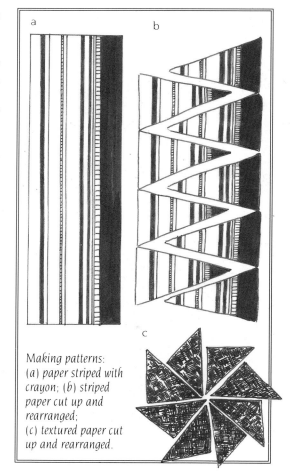

Making patterns:
(a) paper striped with crayon; (b) striped paper cut up and rearranged;
(c) textured paper cut up and rearranged.

Sponge or brush the paint on paper and then cut this up and rearrange the pieces. This method is good for cutting out the letters of the alphabet or numbers. Remember that the print will appear in reverse.

Cheap patterned paper used for wrapping flowers and patterned paper bags used in shops are often a by-product of the commercial printing of synthetic fabrics. The paper can be used again once the pattern is ironed on to the fabric.

Transfer paints and crayons are useful because you can easily see what you are going to print.

Using fabric crayon to create design.

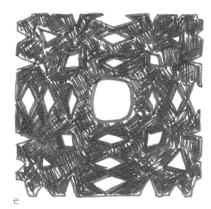

Resulting fabric made into a cushion and quilted. Julie Breden.

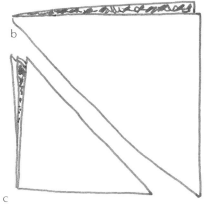

Patterns with textured paper: (a) paper; (b) fold diagonally; (c) fold into quarters; (d) cut into the edges; (e) open out.

a

b

c

d

e

Collecting fabrics

Patchwork is a good way to recycle fabrics which might otherwise be thrown away. Make a collection of pieces of fabric which might be useful. These can be left-over scraps from dressmaking or the unworn sections of old clothes. You can buy small lengths of fabrics and fabric remnants, not only from the fabric and home furnishing departments of large stores but sometimes also from tailors and professional dressmakers. Sometimes jumble sales have good quality patterned garments which can be cut up, washed and used. You can even buy fabrics already cut into patches from some suppliers.

Keep all the pieces of fabric you dye, paint and print by hand: you never know when they will come in useful. It is easier to make a collection if you work with friends or belong to a group, then you can share the fabric pieces.

Before starting to sew have a good look at the various fabrics and try to decide what fibres have been used to make up each one and how they have been constructed. Note the different colours and how texture can alter colour. Is the fabric patterned? What is the dominant colour? Notice particularly the tone of each piece. Is it dark, light or medium?

Sorting

There are many ways of sorting fabrics for storage. They can simply be divided into colour groups, red, orange, yellow, green, blue, indigo and violet, in which case the patterned fabrics can be stored in the group with their dominant colour. However, some people prefer to store their various patterned fabrics together, keeping plain-coloured fabrics separate. See-through fabrics like chiffon and organza, bits of silk and satin, velvet and corduroy, glitzy fabrics and felt can all be stored separately.

Fabrics can also be kept in fibre groups: all cottons, all silks, all synthetics, for example. This is useful if you intend to make a patchwork to wear or use. But there is no reason why fabrics should not be stored together just because they look good together. There is nothing more beautiful and inspiring than a selection of matching and contrasting fabrics.

If you have a design in mind you can collect the fabrics you need over months or even years, keeping them until you have

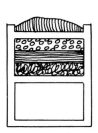

Storage.

enough – and enough time to begin. Store in plastic envelopes with the details of your design so you can see at a glance what you have collected.

Storage

Try to keep fabrics tidy, then they take up less space. Small pieces can be divided into colour groups and stored in washed plastic sweet jars, small plastic bags or plastic envelopes. Fabrics which have been ironed can be arranged in stacking boxes of the sort sold for tools or toys at hardware shops and DIY centres.

People evolve their own methods of storing fabrics but it is a good idea to keep looking through your collection to see what you have, as it is easy to forget. In any case, the colours and colour combinations are often a source of inspiration: by just sorting through a heap of fabrics you can come up with quite new ideas for combining colours and patterns.

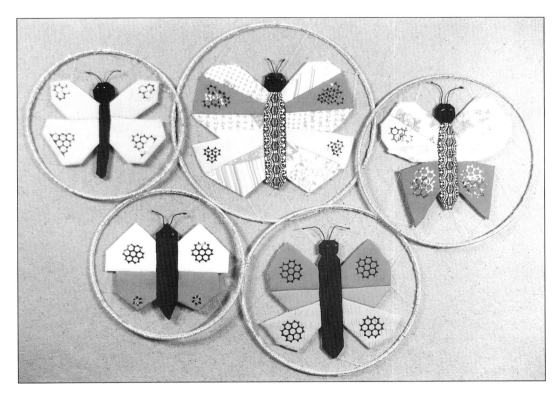

Butterflies: fabric sewn round paper shapes and joined together. Winchester Group 2: Rachel Price, Quita Jones, M.L. Withington, Kirsten Sheill, Heidi Jones.

Paper and markers for design

Designing with paper is quick and easy and you will get a good idea from the design whether the pattern is going to work out well in fabric. Always do several different designs so that you can choose the best one to work on.

Keep all your designs in a folder or several folders in a file. Pin small pieces of the fabrics which you want to use beside the design as you go. Go back over the designs at frequent intervals, adding and altering ideas. There are different methods of designing for patchwork using paper.

Paper

The paper represents the fabric so you need to collect paper in a range of tones. You can start by using black paper to represent dark tones, grey paper to represent medium tones and white paper to represent pale tones.

If you want to use colours, always think in terms of tone as well. Any paper will do, and you can make your own coloured or patterned paper with crayons or pens, pencils or paint. You can also use paper from magazines. You can even use newspaper. Look at parts of the newspaper through half-closed eyes to find the very dark, medium and light tones of print.

Graph paper

Graph paper has a drawn grid pattern. Most regular geometric shapes used in patchwork can be accurately drawn on either squared or isometric graph paper and you can also use this paper to make irregular patterns. Graph paper printed on tracing paper is very useful. Books and sheets of graph paper are available from stationers and newsagents.

Markers

You could buy hundreds of different markers in the form of lead pencils, felt-tip pens, ink pens, chalks, wax crayons, watercolour pencils and so on, but to begin with a black felt tip pen and a lead pencil used on white or pale paper will give three tones, dark, medium and pale. You can then assemble more markers as you need them.

Other equipment

Scissors: keep one pair for cutting paper and a separate pair for cutting fabric.

Glue is useful not only for sticking patterns on paper but also for sticking fabric on paper or on to another fabric if you are making a collage. Use a glue which is suitable for both. PVA medium is good for most things, or use wallpaper paste, which can be mixed up a little at a time. Anything which has been glued should be left to dry thoroughly.

Cutting board and craft knife: a cutting board marked out with a grid of measured lines is very useful for cutting paper templates and for re-cutting blocks of sewn patchwork which need to be squared up. A lino tile makes a good substitute.

Ruler, set square, protractor and compasses can all prove very useful in preparing a design.

The design method you use depends on the type of patchwork you are doing. Suggestions are made at the beginning of each method described.

How to make and use a template

Why use a template at all?

Cut a number of squares free-hand out of paper. Stick them down on a background and note how some edges will not meet and others will overlap, however careful you are. This may look lovely if you are just making a design or a collage picture, but if you want the pieces to lie flat when you sew them together they must fit exactly or you will have gaps and humps. The shapes have to be accurate if they are to lie flat. The best way of achieving this is to make sure the patches are exactly the right shape and size. You can do this by using a template.

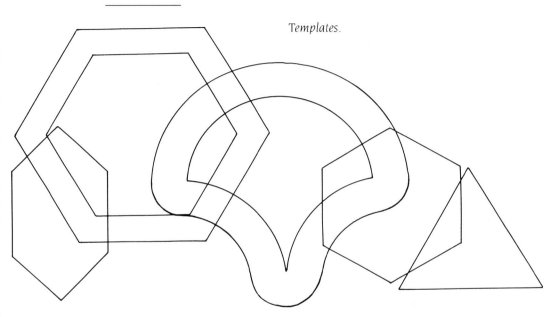

Templates.

Commercial templates

You can buy sets of patchwork templates in most interlocking geometric shapes at large stores and haberdashers. They come in a variety of sizes.

Some templates are in sets of two. One is a metal geometric shape. The other is a plastic window the same size as the metal shape plus a seam allowance. (This allows enough fabric for a seam to turn in to prevent the edges fraying.)

Some templates have a hole in the middle rather than a separate shape. The hole corresponds with the metal shape and the whole template corresponds with the window shape.

Making templates

If you want a size of template not available in the shops, or if you do not want to buy one, you can make your own.

Draw the geometric shape on graph paper. (Most shapes can be drawn out on either squared or isometric graph paper.) The shape should be big enough to include a seam allowance of 6mm all the way round. Stick the graph paper shape to card, or to sandpaper which will cling to the fabric and help to hold the template in place as you work.

Cut out the shape carefully using a craft knife and steel rule. You must be as accurate as possible. A slight mistake at this stage will multiply like a computer virus!

You can also make geometric shapes such as squares, rectangles and diamonds on paper with a ruler, compasses and a set square. Stick to card as above and cut out.

Templates can be used over and over again.

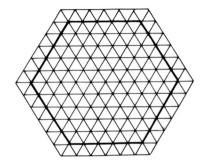

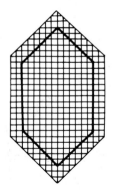

Templates with seam allowance: (top) isometric graph paper; (bottom) squared graph paper.

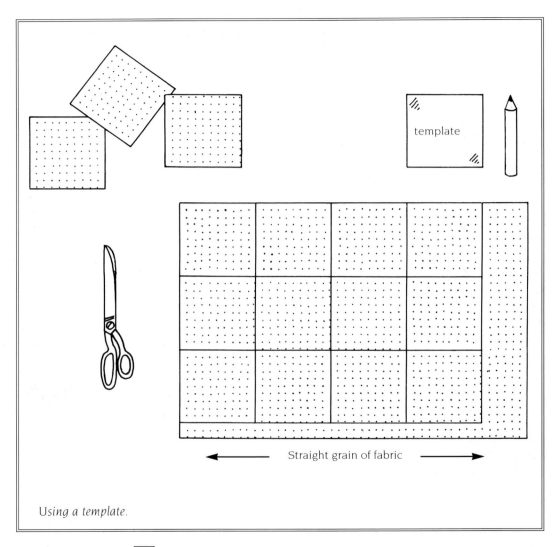

template

Straight grain of fabric

Using a template.

Using templates and cutting out

Method 1

For simple regular shapes with no curves, for example, rectangles, squares, triangles and diamonds, place the template with the seam allowance on the straight grain of the fabric. If you are using a template with a window it is possible to choose exactly the right area of pattern on the fabric. Using a hard pencil or a fabric marker, draw round the template and cut out the patch.

Method 2

Some shapes, for example clam shells, hexagons and irregular shapes for a picture, need a paper template as well as a fabric patch. Use a metal template to cut out a paper pattern for each patch. Use strong brown paper or the backs of old greetings cards for these.

Place the metal template on the paper and cut out. Use a craft knife or scissors rather than drawing round and then cutting out. Make sure the table is protected or use a cutting mat.

Use the template with the seam allowance to cut out the fabric patches. It is a good idea to cut out a supply of paper templates and fabric patches before you begin to sew.

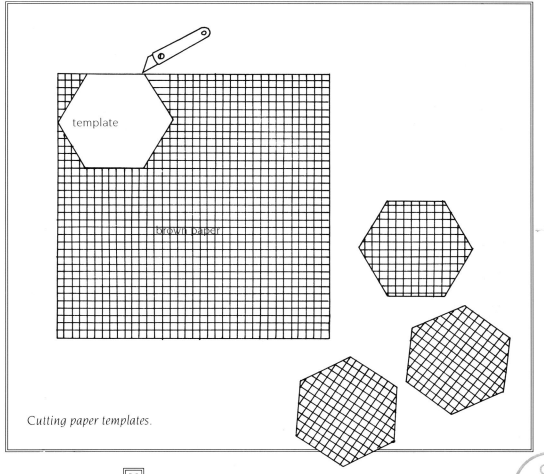

template

brown paper

Cutting paper templates.

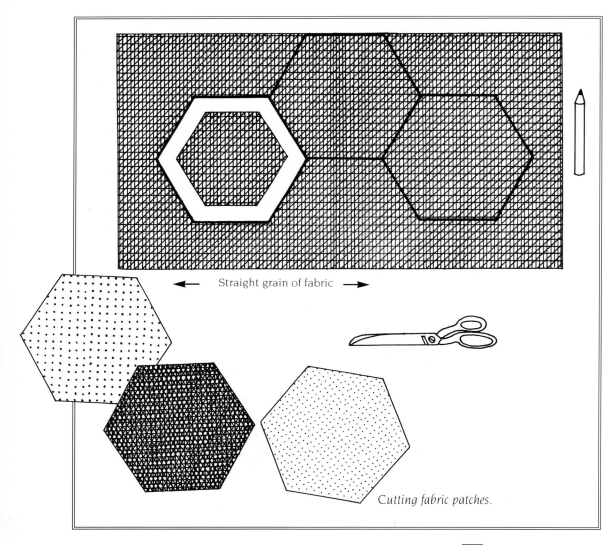

Straight grain of fabric ←→

Cutting fabric patches.

Pin a paper template to the back of each patch. Pull the edges round evenly and tack with tacking cotton. Start with a knot and finish with two stitches. You will pull these stitches out eventually.

If you are using the commercial template with the hole in the middle, draw through the hole to make paper templates, and round the outside for the fabric patch to go with it. If you are using graph paper, you can make one template for the paper patterns and another which includes a seam allowance for the fabric patches.

You can buy commercial iron-on patchwork patterns. These are patchwork shapes printed on iron-on interfacing. Cut out the patches, iron them on, then sew along the dotted lines.

Paper patterns can be made in any shape, covered with fabric and then sewn together. Draw the picture on paper. Divide with a ruler, or free-hand but try to make sure shapes are fairly big, with not too many sharp angles.

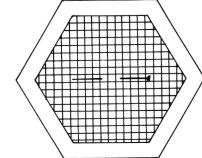

a

Sewing the patchwork

Basic equipment

Patchwork can be done by hand or with a sewing machine. A basic sewing kit for any textile work should include stainless steel pins, sharp scissors (keep a pair to use with textiles only) and a variety of needles. Generally, blunt or tapestry needles are used to do canvas and counted thread work where the needle goes between the weave of the fabric. Sharp needles are required for most other fabrics and techniques including patchwork. Use a needle the right size for the thread – not too big and not too small – and never use more than approximately 30cm (12in) of thread at a time.

Keep the sewing kit together in a box.

Sewing machine

All you need is a machine that will do straight stitch; electric, hand and treadle machines are all suitable for patchwork. However, it is important that the machine works properly. This means that the stitches are even and flat on both sides. The stitches should be firm so they do not pull out.

Always try out the machine before you start work, using a piece of similar fabric.

Iron

Have iron and ironing board to hand so you can press the work frequently to keep it flat. If the pieces have been machined together, press the seams open where possible. If they have been hand sewn, press them neatly to one side to give a little extra strength.

How to join the patches together

The method you use depends on whether you are making something to wear or use, or whether you want to make something decorative, to hang on the wall for instance.

Sewing by machine

Rectangles, squares, triangle and diamond-shaped patches are easy to sew by machine. Use sewing thread to match the patchwork fabric and use the same thread in the bobbin. Set the machine to straight stitch and use a medium stitch setting.

Pin, then tack, patches with right sides

(a-d) Tacking fabric shapes to paper template.

b

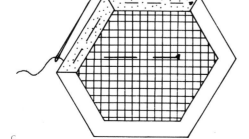

c

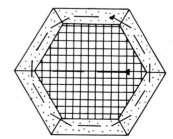

d

together. (If you pin with the pins at right angles to the line of machine stitches there is often no need to tack.)

Either machine, using the machine foot as a guide for the seam allowance (6mm, ¼in), or measure and draw the seam allowance with a fabric marker or a hard pencil. (Do not use biro as the mark is almost impossible to remove.) Then sew along the line. There is no need to tie off the ends of the thread but cut them off neatly.

It is much easier to sew patches together by machine if you first sew them in strips, and then sew the strips together.

Sewing by hand

Patches without paper patterns: Measure and draw the seam allowance as above and sew along the line with running stitches. Start and finish securely.

Patches with paper patterns: Place patches with their right sides facing and oversew along one edge. When you have finished, remove the papers. They can be used again.

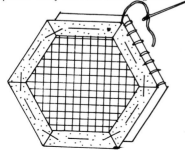

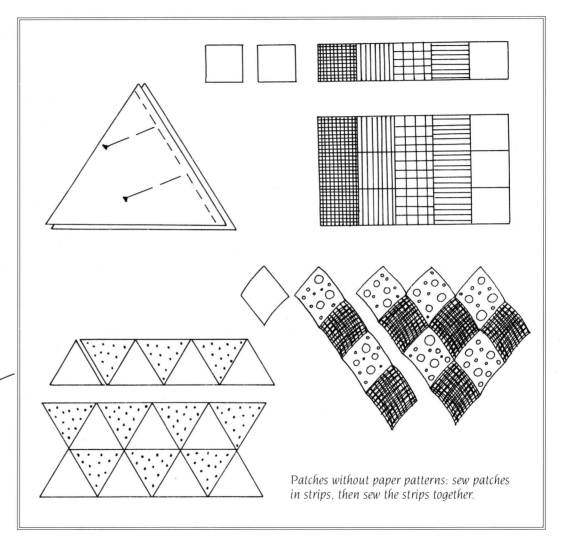

Patches without paper patterns: sew patches in strips, then sew the strips together.

TYPES OF PATCHWORK

Types of patchwork

The shape and arrangement of the fabric patches produce many different patterns and types of patchwork. Some can be done by machine while others can only be done by hand. People are still inventing new ways of putting patchwork shapes together.

Hand methods always take longer but you can combine a small piece of hand patchwork with machine patchwork by sewing it on or including it in the larger machine patchwork.

A group of people can make one large patchwork between them by making one square each, then sewing them all together. Keep to shapes which will fit together easily such as squares, diamonds and rectangles.

For each type of patchwork you will need to think of three things, the method, the design and the fabrics.

The method

Start by doing a small practice piece just to see how it is done and to make sure that there are no problems with the size of the patches, the overall measurements, whether the fabrics sew or stick easily, and so on. Use pieces of spare fabric to practise and keep the sample in a folder with your design pinned to a piece of paper with your comments.

The design

There are various ways of designing a patchwork depending upon the type you have chosen but make sure you are quite happy with your design before you begin to cut out the fabric.

It is always a good idea to do several designs before you decide on the one you prefer. You can save the others in a folder; they may be useful later. Look at your design from a distance as well as close up to make sure that the tones of the colours make the sort of pattern you want.

The fabrics

Choose the fabrics as you design and before you begin sewing to make sure you get just the effect you want. Pin the fabrics in the right order on a board then stand well back so you can see them from a distance.

Do any of the colours spoil the whole design because they are too strong? Do the tones of each of the fabric patches contribute to the pattern? If you are not sure about one of the fabrics, now is the time to be decisive and get rid of it.

If the patchwork is to be used or worn, make sure that the fabrics you pick are all of the same type, for instance all cotton, all wool or all silk. So, be careful – but also be bold! Experiment and try out interesting fabrics like corduroy, velvet, see-through fabrics, wool tweed and satin.

Fabrics for patchwork including tie-dye pieces.
Cushion by Rebecca Hemmings.

Fabric collage

In a collage, the fabrics are stuck to a background. This is ideal for those people who enjoy cutting and arranging the fabric shapes but do not like sewing. A collage can also be used to plan a sewn patchwork, to work out the colours and tones and to give an impression of the final result. You can cut the pieces free-hand or use a template (see page 27).

Background

This needs to be fairly firm to hold all the small pieces adequately. Either use stiff paper or stick a piece of fabric on to paper, thin card or even hardboard with PVA glue or wallpaper paste and allow to dry.

Sticking the patches

Spread the glue on to the background rather than on to the individual pieces, then place the shapes in position with tweezers before pressing down with your fingers. Alternatively, you can dip fabric pieces in wallpaper paste and spread out on the background while they are still wet.

Allow a collage to dry thoroughly. It may need to be weighted down to prevent the patches from lifting.

Try out a variety of different fabrics for collage. Use patches with frayed and fringed edges, and leave some edges raised for effect. You can use paper as well as fabric.

Patchwork collage. Sophie Allchin.

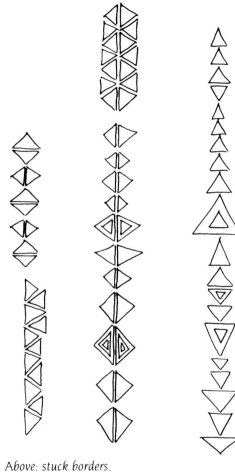

Above: stuck borders.

Right: Nine square: collage of geometric shapes made from hand-dyed cotton fabrics stuck on paper. Exwick Middle School, Exeter.

Patchwork using strips

Several types of patchwork are based on using fabric strips arranged in different patterns. These are all easy to do and can be stuck or sewn by hand or machine.

Strips of fine woven cotton can be torn along the straight grain of the fabric. If the fabric will not tear easily you can sometimes see to cut along the grain. If necessary, make a template (see p.27).

Make sure the strip is wide enough to allow for the seams. Strips much less than 3cm (1¼in) wide are apt to disintegrate, but if you like using very thin strips use ribbon which has a strong selvage down both sides and needs very little seam allowance. 30cm makes an easy-to-manage length but strips can be longer or shorter.

Method

Sew the strips together to make a large rectangle. If you make several the same size, these can also be sewn together in various

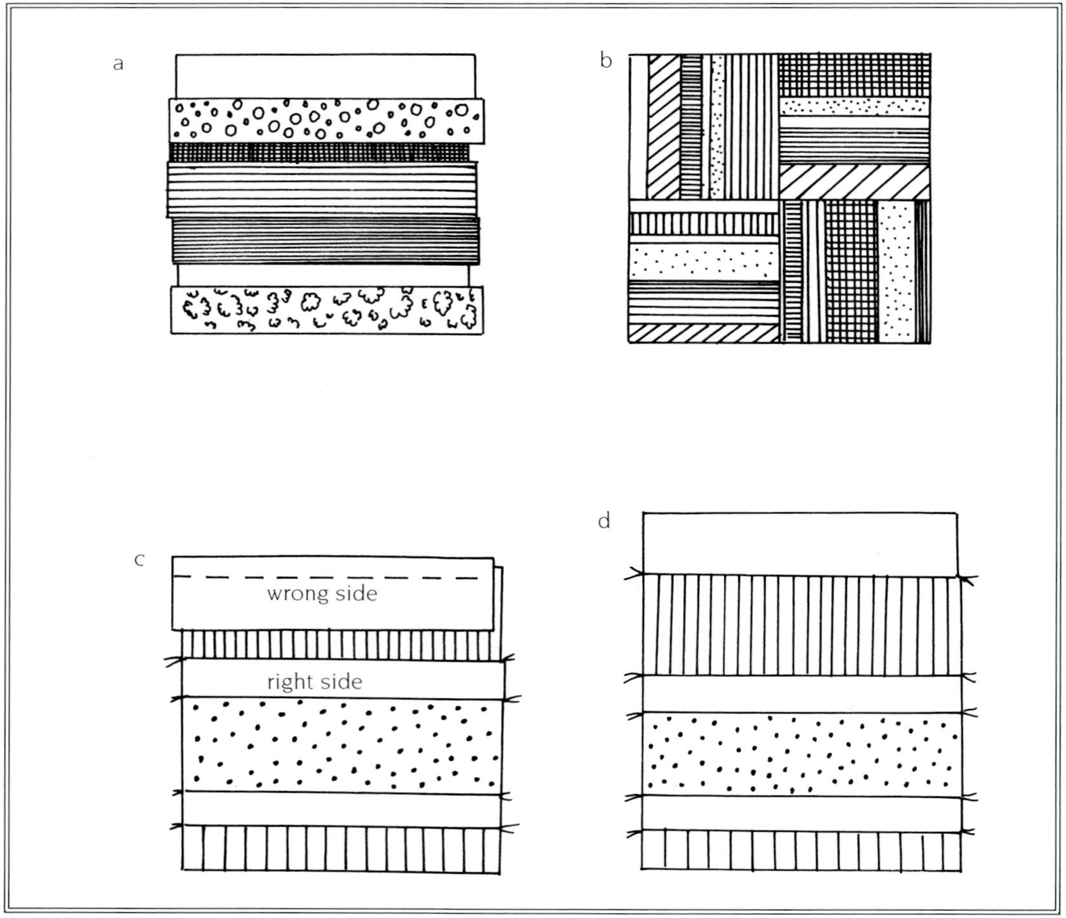

a

b

c

wrong side

right side

d

(a, b) sewing strips together; (c) finished block;
(d) four blocks joined.

patterns. When you have finished sewing trim the edges to size.

Alternatively, you can apply the strips, one at a time, to a piece of cotton or calico.

Design

To work out a design use coloured strips of paper of all kinds. You might try using tones of one colour ranging from dark to light, or alternate dark and light. Look for ideas for colour schemes in commercial fabrics and wrapping papers.

Arrange the strips on paper and, when you are satisfied, stick them down. You can then follow the pattern.

Experiment with pattern. Make six squares exactly the same size. Arrange them to make different patterns by rotating every alternate shape. Or, colour strips on a sheet of lined writing paper. Make some wide and some narrow.

Fabrics

Strip patchwork is very easy to do and can be used to show off all sorts of interesting patterns and combinations of fabric. It is ideal for many of the more unusual – and beautiful – materials such as ribbon and braid, for strips of silk, velvet and lace, and even for strips of knitting and crochet work.

Again, experiment! Use alternate plain and matching patterns, either bought or created by you to order. Print patterns along some strips of fabric and experiment with

Left: Strip patchwork: top stitching and embroidery. Martha Connock.
Right: Strip patchwork: top hand-stitching. Zoe Hartwright.

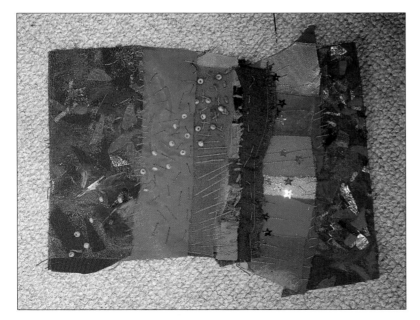

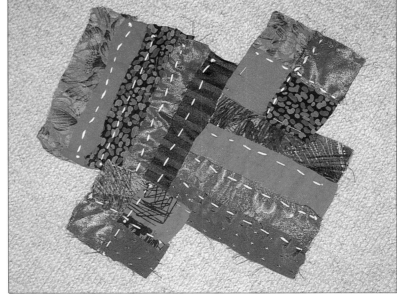

striped fabrics to see what patterns you can create. Strips of tweed in different tones make subtle, warm and hard-wearing patchworks.

Overlap strips and top stitch on the outside so the stitches show and become part of the design. If you do this, search out interesting threads, metallics or random-dyed types, for instance.

Left: Strip patchwork: top stitching and embroidery. Charlotte Davies.

Right: Detail of patchwork quilt (see p. 84). Dyed and printed fabrics: top to bottom, a) dyed and sponged, b) potato prints, c) dyed then printed using sticky-backed plastic squares as resist, d) tie-dye, e) as a), f) as c), g) as b), h) as d).

Seminole patchwork

The Seminole Indians of North America developed this way of manipulating strip patchwork at the end of the nineteenth century. For this type of patchwork strips of fabric are joined to make a large rectangle. This is then cut into strips again, this time at right angles to the stripes. Finally, the cut pieces are rearranged and sewn together.

Method

Sew together four or five 30cm (12in) strips. These need not all be the same width. Lay a wide ruler at right angles to the stripes and mark out a new set of strips with a water-soluble pen. Make these wide enough for a seam allowance of 6mm (¼in).

Cut and arrange the strips to make a pattern. Pin, tack and sew them together. More, different patterns can be made by cutting at different angles, for instance at 45°.

Design

To work out a design use striped paper. You can make this yourself by sticking paper or fabric strips on to a background, or paint or crayon stripes on paper. Remember to contrast light with dark and medium tones of colour. You can also use striped wrapping paper which makes interesting patterns.

Fabrics

Use woven fabrics for things to wear. Contrasting plain fabrics are often effective. Small patterned fabrics add texture. However, for really exciting textures go for strips of ribbon and silk or corduroy and needlecord.

Seminole techniques.

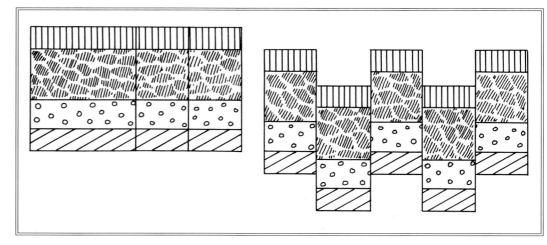

Hanging: Seminole patchwork with hand-dyed
fabrics. Compton C. of E. Primary School, Berks.

Log cabin patchwork

The log cabin method is used in many areas of the world, including China and Canada. This is but one of its many different names. In log cabin work, fabric strips are sewn round a central fabric square to form a large square.

Method

Cut a fabric square, using a template (see p.27). Sew the first strip along one edge of the square. Trim it at both ends so that the strip is the same width as the square. Sew the second strip along the adjacent side and trim.

Keep working round in this way, adding strips and trimming the ends, until the square is as big as you need it to be. You can join up several squares to make a large rectangle. This will create another pattern.

Design

Use strips of light- and dark-toned paper to make patterns. Arrange alternately two light,

Right: Log cabin techniques.

Far right: Quilt by Jan Hassard: log cabin quilt using small printed fabrics. Note over-all pattern created by the position of the blocks.

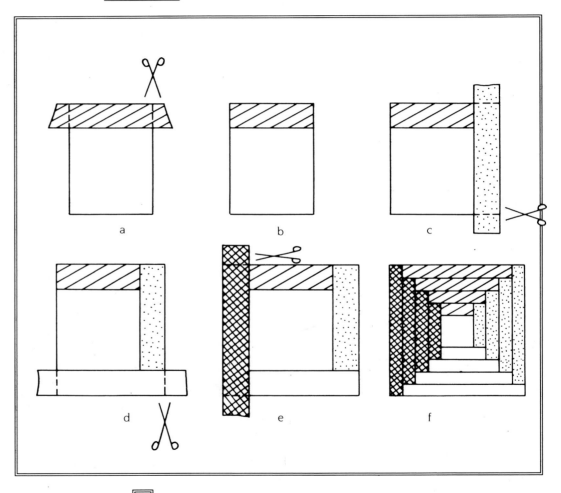

a

b

c

d

e

f

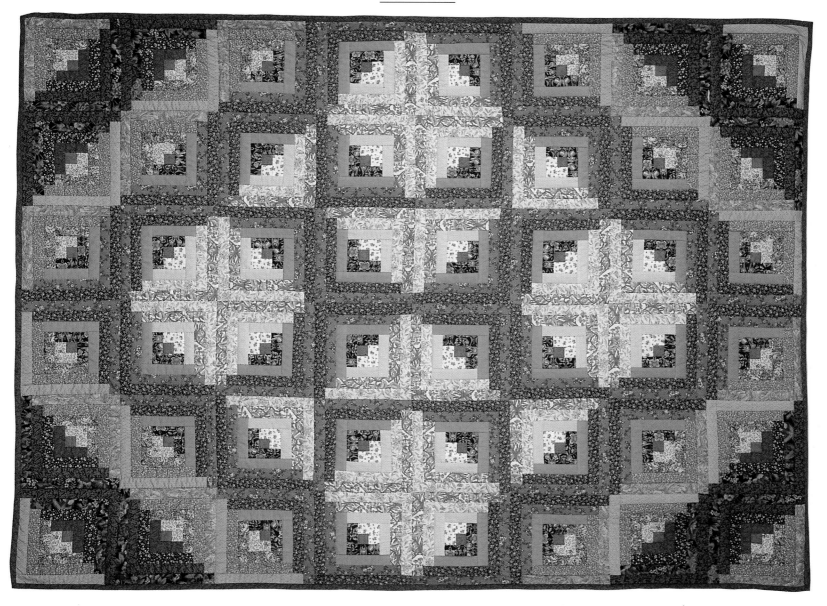

then two dark strips round the central square, which can be either light or dark. Or, arrange four light, then four dark around a central light or dark square.

Draw out your patterns on squared graph paper. Make a number of each of these patterns and arrange and rearrange to make different overall patterns.

Fabrics

Use woven fabrics or ribbons, plain and printed cottons. Try pieces of silk or shot silk and notice how the light changes the pattern. Strips of see-through fabric such as organza or chiffon could be top-stitched with silver thread.

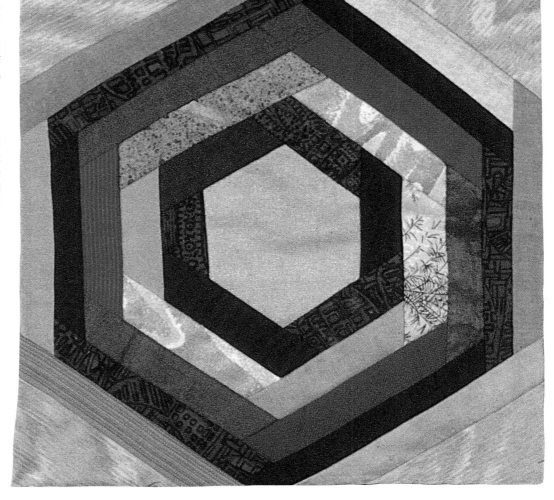

Left: *Log cabin patchwork hanging, each block sewn round a canvas work square. Bluecoat C. of E. Primary School, Wotton-under-Edge, Glos. Right: Log cabin worked round a hexagon (detail of p.80). Alice Timmins.*

47

Patchwork using geometric shapes

Block patterns or American block

This type of patchwork was worked extensively by the early settlers in North America. It can be sewn on a machine or by hand. The block or square is divided symmetrically into triangles and squares, and coloured with contrasting tones. When the blocks are put together, even more patterns are created.

Design

Use a square of paper to make a block about 15cm (6in) square. Fold this into three, open and fold into three the other way so that you end up with nine smaller squares.

With a pencil and ruler, or by folding, divide some of the squares diagonally to make a symmetrical pattern and colour in some of the shapes with a dark-coloured pencil or pen. You can also make patterns by folding the squares of paper into 4, 9, 12 or 16.

There is almost an infinite number of ways of folding and colouring these patterns, using pale, medium and dark tones. Many of the patterns have names given to them by the early American settlers, for example Crazy Ann, Handy Andy and California Star.

Make four blocks exactly the same and put these together. Notice how yet another pattern is formed.

Other ideas:

a| Use two squares of contrasting paper (e.g. black and white) folded in the same way. Cut out the shapes. Exchange shapes to make two patterns.

b| Using squared graph paper, a ruler and pencil, experiment with different ways of dividing a square.

c| You can make a see-through patchwork by folding and dividing a square of a fabric such as felt. Tack the pieces to a piece of see-through fabric, for instance organza, then lay another piece of the see-through fabric over the top. Stitch round the shapes going through all three layers.

d| If you have a computer with a design program based on grid patterns, you will be able to design with that.

Note that even the most complicated patterns are made up of only one, two or three basic shapes, usually a triangle, a square or a rectangle.

Colour in your designs with crayons, paints or felt-tip pens, using contrasting tones.

Make an accurate template in the size

Hanging: shadow-work patches. The patterns in individual squares are made by folding and cutting up 30 cm (12 in) felt squares and rearranging the pieces. Preston Young Textile Group.

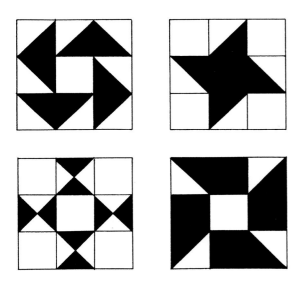

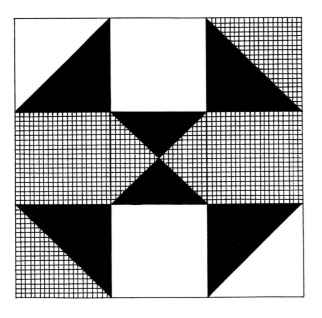

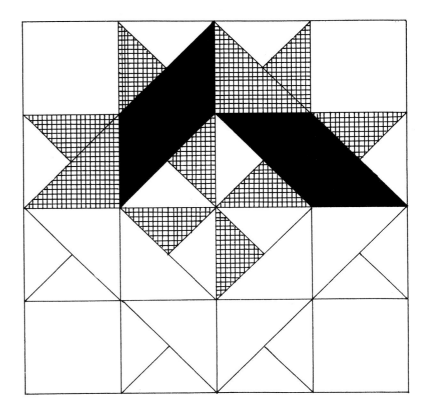

American block patterns.

you want for each basic shape, on squared graph paper. Remember to include a seam allowance.

Fabrics

The early American settlers were very short of goods and made full use of every scrap of patterned or plain fabric available. They knew the real meaning of having to recycle old clothes and furnishings. Some of their quilts, though made in hardship and from necessity, are real works of art, with beautiful, complicated patterns, created by using fabrics in contrasting tones. There is a collection well worth seeing in the American Museum in Bath. Choose contrasting woven

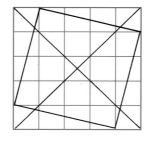

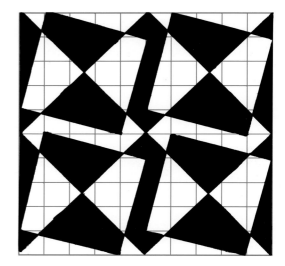

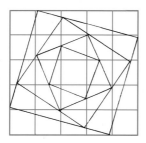

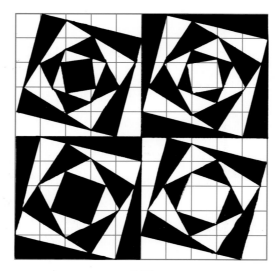

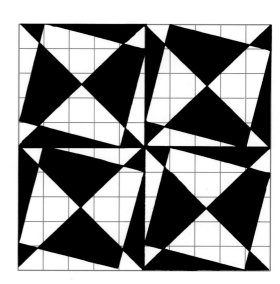

Experiments dividing squares.

fabrics. These might be bought especially for the purpose or hand-dyed or patterned. If you are making an appliqué or a collage piece, try either hand-made or commercial felt.

Method

Use a piece of light and a piece of dark woven cotton to make a sample. Cut out the correct number of pieces for one block using a template. Arrange the pieces in strips. Pin and/or tack, then sew the strips together. Press.

You can sew similar blocks together to make a large pattern, or alternate blocks with plain-coloured fabric squares. Or, you can use one block as the middle square for a log cabin patchwork. Try out different layouts for yourself.

When similar blocks are joined another pattern is formed: microwave-dyed fabrics.

Patchwork mosaic or English patchwork

This is probably one of the most common types of patchwork and examples can be seen in all parts of the world. One, or perhaps two geometric shapes are used to create the pattern.

Regular polygons – the square, the equilateral triangle and the hexagon – will interlock to form an all-over tesselation in two dimensions. Other semi-regular polygons need an additional shape to cover an area completely, without leaving spaces. These shapes are all used in patchwork mosaic. The pattern in this case comes from the colours and contrasting tones of the patches.

Design

There are many different ways of designing a mosaic, so try them all.

Graph paper: Use both squared graph paper and isometric graph paper, noting which geometric shapes fit into squared graph paper and which into the isometric graph paper. Spend some time just outlining shapes, noticing how they interlock, and how other shapes are formed.

Decide which pattern you want to concentrate on and fill in some of the shapes with a felt-tip pen, leaving some blank. You will see that the empty shapes contrast with the filled shapes to make a pattern. It is the contrast between the tones that creates the pattern.

Go on to use three tones, for instance a lead pencil and a black felt-tip pen to fill in some of the shapes, while leaving some blank. The pencil gives a medium tone, the felt-tip pen gives a dark tone and the blank gives a pale tone.

Right: Patchwork tree with applied flowers and hand embroidery. East Kent Young Textile Group. Far right: Dancing dolls: fabric sewn round paper shapes. Rebecca Sumpter, Fiona Beck, Caroline Grey, Eleonor Welch.

Below: Regular polygons: squares, hexagons, equilateral triangles.

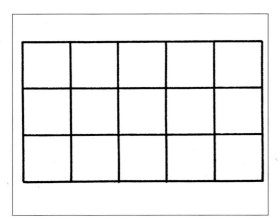

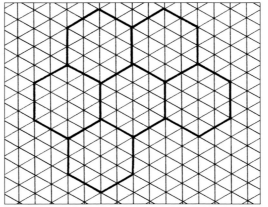

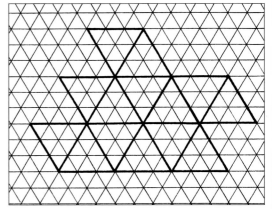

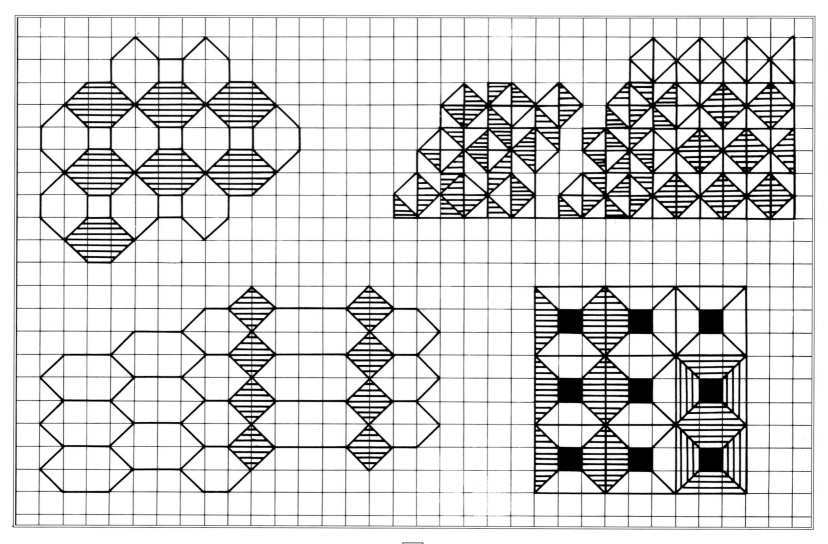

Try different tonal schemes using the same pattern by putting dark instead of light, medium instead of dark, and so on. Note what a difference this makes. You can also fill in some shapes with patterns, stripes, spots, criss-crosses for instance, to contrast with plain colours. Use pencils, paint or ink to colour in the patterns.

The effect of the pattern you create can be easily seen if you look at it with your eyes half-closed or stand back to view it from a distance.

Cut paper: Cut out coloured paper shapes and arrange them to make an interlocking pattern. Try both free-hand cutting and using a hand-made or a commercial template. If you cut free-hand, try to make the geometric shapes more or less the same size. You can cut several at a time from folded paper. Use coloured or patterned paper in two or three tones of one or two colours.

Notice that the pattern on paper has a predominant colour and tone, just like fabric. Paper with a small regular pattern is easy to use but you can also cut out definite motifs to include in a pattern. Use all types of paper to get the effect you want – wrapping paper, sweet paper and silver paper, or colour your own.

Left: Patterns on squared graph paper.
Right: Patterns on isometric graph paper.

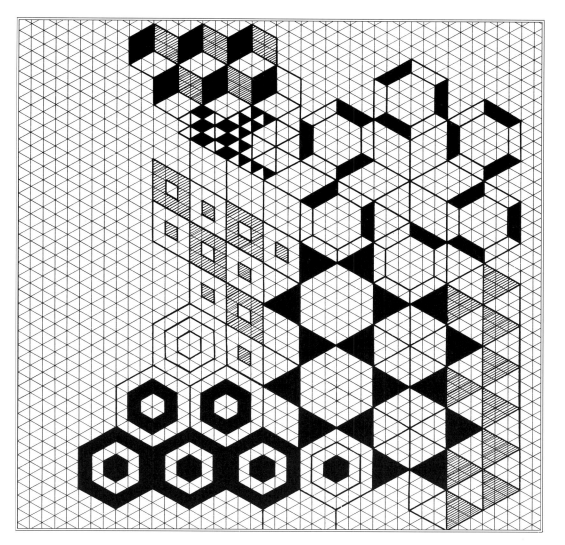

Make patterns, and then stick down any design you particularly like. Keep in mind the tones of the colours used and make sure they contrast with each other, even if the contrast is only subtle.

Printing: Block printing is a good way of making an interlocking pattern, using geometric shapes such as squares, triangles and diamonds. Cut the shape you want to reproduce into the surface of a halved potato, or cut a piece of card or foam (see p.17).

Use paint or ink on a wad of kitchen paper in a saucer. Dip the cut-out pattern in the paint and press on to the paper to make a print. Notice the similarities between block printing and patchwork.

Collecting: There are many patterns in the man-made environment which you can make use of. Floors are particularly good. Tiled pavements in old churches and abbeys are a fine source of inspiration as indeed is modern patterned paving. The pattern of building bricks and stones, ceramic wall tiles, parts of stained glass windows and metal structures are often made up of tessellated patterns. Look for books on mosaic floor and wall patterns, especially Roman and Arab. Cities are full of patterns on buildings.

Look for patterns in the natural environment too. Fruits like pineapple, pine cones and sunflower seeds all make interlocking patterns. Can you find others?

There are so many different ways of creating patchwork patterns and so many colours and combinations of colours and patterns, that you can create an infinite variety. Save designs in a folder, even if you never do turn them into a fabric patchwork.

Fabrics

Use the same weight and type of fabric for the pieces of any patchwork which is to be worn or used. Use different patterned fabrics from the same colour group. Link plain and patterned fabric through their colours.

Hexagons: synthetic fabric coloured with transfer paint (see p.22).

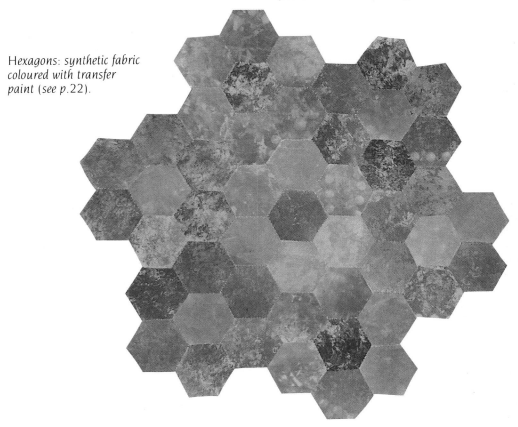

Stripes, both printed, woven and in corduroy, are interesting to work with because they can be turned to make different patterns. Shot silk has one colour weft and another coloured warp so that its colour changes depending on the direction of the light. Again, turn the patches for the best effect.

Velvets and silks will go well together (as long as they are the same weight). They can also be embroidered. Try groups of dark, rich colours and groups of pale, ethereal colours. Black and white make a dramatic contrast. You can achieve striking contrasts with some colours and gentle ones with others. It is possible to get a contrast even if the colours are fairly near in tone.

Method

You can sew squares and rectangles, triangles and diamonds by machine or by hand. For other shapes such as hexagons, sew round paper templates then sew by hand. Cut the patches and arrange in order then sew as described on p. 32.

English patchwork using hexagons and triangles. Note how just the right piece of fabric has been chosen for the patches. Detail of the Blossom quilt (see p.85).

Variations – making your own patterns

Jigsaw patchwork

You can turn any picture or pattern or large shape into a patchwork.

Method

Draw the picture and divide it into sections. Try to keep these simple and fairly big. If they are too small they will drop to bits. Try not to have too many acute angles.

When you are satisfied, trace off the picture on to tracing paper. Cut this up and use the pieces as paper templates (see p. 29). Make up as English patchwork.

Put-and-take

With put-and-take you can make more complicated shapes which will fit together to make an interlocking pattern.

To experiment, cut a square from a piece of squared graph paper. Cut into one edge, and add the cut piece to one of the other edges to make an irregular shape. (Shapes without very sharp corners are most suitable.) Use this shape as a template and cut several out of paper to see how they fit

Patchwork butterflies (see also p.25)

together. In this way, quite intricate designs can be made, some of which will be suitable for patchwork.

To sew the patchwork

Make paper templates, cover with fabric and sew together. Or, cut the shapes in fabric backed with bondaweb and iron to a background fabric such as cotton or calico. Sew down using one of the appliqué methods on p.62.

Use fabrics which will not fray, such as felt or leather.

Put-and-take patchwork design. Josephine Davison.

Put-and-take design on isometric graph paper.

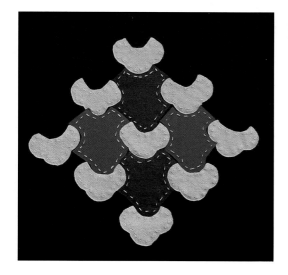

Put-and-take patchwork design. Joanna Mawby

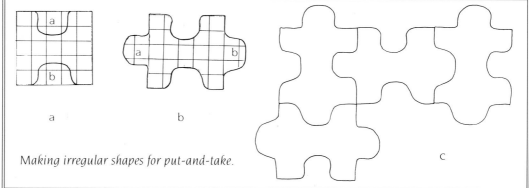

Making irregular shapes for put-and-take.

Pixels

On television, the faces of people who do not want to be identified are sometimes shown as a mass of coloured squares. These are called pixels. Some colour photocopiers have a programme which will turn a colour photograph into a pattern of pixels. These patterns can be used as an exciting basis for a patchwork design.

It is also possible to do more or less the same thing with coloured pencils or crayons, by hand.

Method

Use a sheet of graph tracing paper and a suitable photograph. Place the paper squarely on the photograph, and try to decide which is the dominant colour within each square. Colour it in.

It is a good idea to try several and choose the best, rather than just using the first one.

As the shapes produced are either square or rectangular they can be sewn together easily either by hand or by machine. The designs can also be used for both collage and appliqué.

Silk appliqué (see p.62) based on a pixel pattern.

Right: Photograph enlarged on a colour photocopier.
Far right: The same photograph turned into pixels.

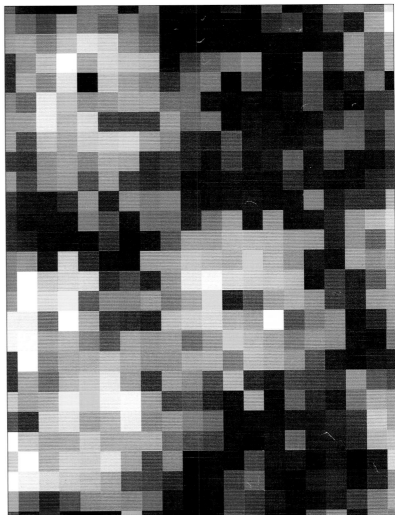

Appliqué

Appliqué means applying cut-out fabric shapes to another piece of fabric and stitching them down. If several pictures are joined to make a large piece of work, each background piece must interlock.

The background

This can be just one piece of fabric, two or three strips or a mosaic of small pieces.

If you are using just one piece of fabric, it should be strengthened with another piece of fabric such as cotton, calico or interlining. Sew or bond this to the back.

The extra fabric will also support the background and keep the work flat.

If you are using strips, or a mosaic of fabric, these should also be sewn, bonded or stuck to another piece of fabric or interlining. Overlap the pieces as you sew them on like crazy patchwork (see p.71).

Applying the pieces

There are several methods of applying the fabric pieces to the background. If you are making something to wear or use, the appliqué needs to be firmly attached so that the pieces of fabric don't come adrift during

washing or cleaning. This is not so important in a picture or hanging, where all sorts of exciting fabrics can be stuck or sewn on and left to hang, with raw edges, fraying out, and so on.

Choose the method which you find easiest and which best suits your project.

Turned-in edges: Each fabric piece should be big enough to turn in the edge without its disintegrating. You can add fine details later with stitching.

Different backgrounds for appliqué.

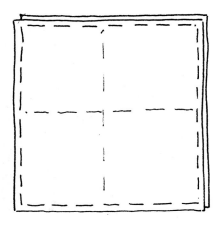

a

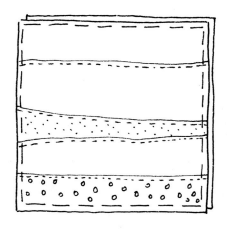

b

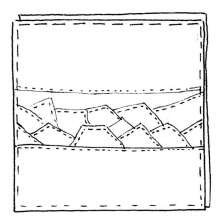

c

Detail of the Blossom quilt (see p.85): applied
shapes with turned-in edges.

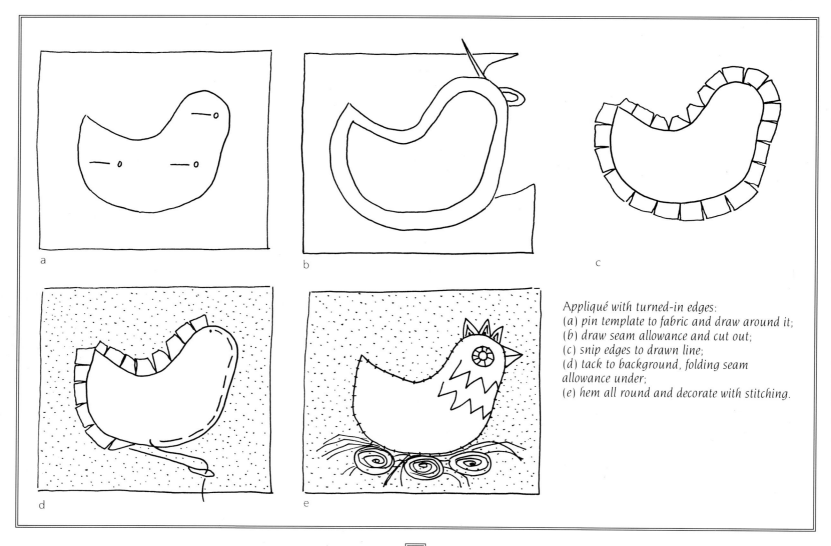

Appliqué with turned-in edges:
(a) pin template to fabric and draw around it;
(b) draw seam allowance and cut out;
(c) snip edges to drawn line;
(d) tack to background, folding seam allowance under;
(e) hem all round and decorate with stitching.

Applied shapes without turnings (*see overleaf*),
machined and decorated with machine embroidery.

Make a paper template of the shape you are going to apply. Pin this on the fabric, keeping the straight grain of the fabric matching the straight grain of the background where you can, so that the piece lies flat. If this is impossible, back the fabric with fine, iron-on interfacing.

Draw round the template with a water-soluble fabric marker, tailors' chalk or a hard pencil. Mark a seam allowance of 6mm (¼in). Cut out.

Snip the edges into the outer curves and cut Vs into the inner curves. This allows you to turn in the edges without creasing.

Pin the shapes to the background and stitch either by hand with hem stitch or by machine with straight stitch.

Without turnings: Proceed as above, but without leaving a seam allowance.

Pin, then tack, the shapes to the background, then stitch round. You can use hem stitch, then cover the edge with a line of embroidery stitches. If you use a machine, sew round each shape with straight stitch, then cover the line of stitches with close zig-zag or satin stitch.

Other methods: Stick the pieces on with bondaweb or a fabric glue applied sparingly to the background and then stitch. If you use this method, the stitches are not so important for actually holding the fabric so make interesting stitch patterns.

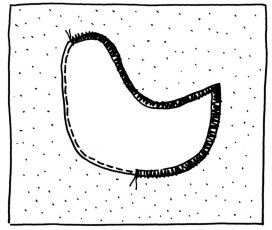

Appliqué shape, machined with straight stitch, then zigzag.

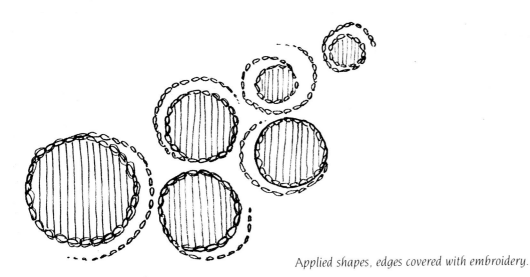

Applied shapes, edges covered with embroidery.

Below: Row of houses: individual houses made as strip patchwork, one strip each for the sky, the roof and the walls. Walls decorated with fabric markers; windows applied with bondaweb and sewn; embroidered decoration. Breckfield Junior School, Liverpool.

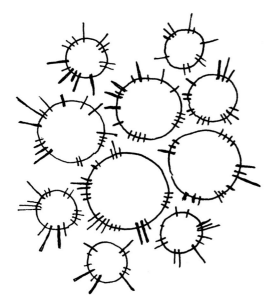

Applied shapes, decorated with stitch patterns.

Machine stitch through the applied pieces from top to bottom and side to side instead of sewing round each one in turn. This is particularly useful for catching down small pieces. It is most suitable for pictures. Use either straight or zig-zag stitch or a mixture of both. Try different coloured machine threads.

Left: Patchwork shapes and stitches built up to make an exciting decorative surface. Martha Connock.

Leave raw edges and fringes to create texture. Fine and non-fray fabrics can often be caught down with just one stitch.
Pin or lightly glue the pieces in position between two pieces of see-through fabric such as organdie, organza or chiffon before sewing.

Design

Think about how the item you are making is

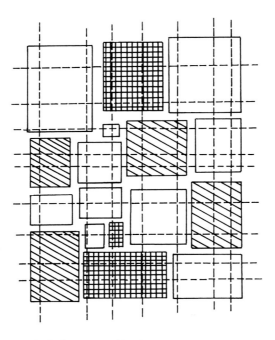

Applied shapes, machined.

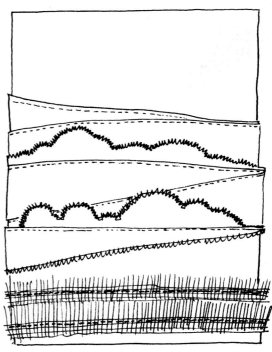

Applied shapes, using straight and zigzag stitches.

to be used when you choose materials and techniques. For instance, appliqué is often used for large pieces of work such as hangings and banners which will mainly be seen and must be visible from a distance. So use bold, simple shapes in the design, and keep looking at the work from some way away as well as close up as you work.

Fabrics

Most fabric is quite hard-wearing. You might need to back flimsy fabrics with interfacing or bondaweb but don't hesitate to make use of fabrics like silks and velvets, chiffons and organzas which create lovely effects when superimposed. You can cut shapes of flowers, leaves and other small things from printed fabrics for appliqué work or add small details by embroidering over.

Individual appliqué rectangles were joined to make a hanging. Young Textile Group, Portsmouth.

Crazy patchwork

This is a form of appliqué using irregular geometric shapes. Fabric shapes are built up gradually to cover the background completely. Use a firm woven fabric as background and sew on the first shape. Overlap the next shape and sew down. Continue overlapping shapes and sewing until the background is completely covered. Different-sized shapes can be used.

Fabrics

Crazy patchwork was very popular in Victorian times, and used to be done in velvets and silks, which were then embroidered all round the edge and decorated with sprigs of embroidered flowers.

It is very important to choose similar types of fabric for a piece of work, for example all printed cotton, all silk and velvet, all shot silk, or all satin. The colours are also important and should be carefully chosen before beginning. It is a good idea to have a colour theme, perhaps all rich dark colours, or all pastel colours, or printed cottons with the same background colour, or all striped fabrics. Choose colours which go together well.

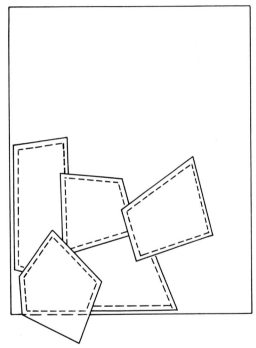

Crazy patchwork techniques.

Detail of crazy patchwork bedspread (see p.77) by Tracy Spencer.

Folded and gathered patchwork

Somerset patchwork

Method

Use squares of fabric about 60cm (24in) square. |a| Fold each in half, with the fold at the top, |b| then fold the top outside corners to the bottom centre, to make a triangle. |c| Press.

Take a piece of background fabric such as calico or cotton. Fold in half, quarters and diagonally into eighths, then press, so that you can see the creases. |d| Arrange four of the folded pieces with the points to the centre of the background fabric. Pin, tack and stitch in position. |e| Arrange the other folded pieces to overlap the edges of the first arrangement, pin, tack and sew. |f| The folded pieces can also be used to create texture.

Alternatively, fold diagonally, then fold again, to get your pad of fabric. Pieces folded by both methods can be used to make a serrated or toothed border.

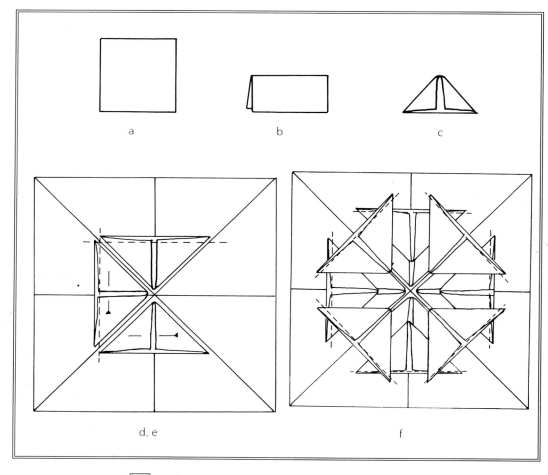

a   b   c

d, e   f

Folded patchwork techniques.

Making a toothed border.

Fabrics

Try different woven cottons, combining plain with patterned and light with dark. This type of patchwork can be used for something quite small so you have the chance to use more exotic fabrics. The points themselves can be as small as you can manage.

Right: Folded patchwork: bat by Nell Humphrey, hedgehog by Penny Grey, owl by Joy Seldon.

Cathedral windows

Method

Try this method with soft cotton or lightweight, well-washed calico, which is not springy.

Cut a number of squares of fabric, 20cm (9in) square. On each square turn in the edges about 6mm (¼in) all the way round and tack. Press. |a| Fold the points to the centre and hold in position with two stitches. |b| Place two folded squares face to face and oversew down one side. Open out with the folded sides uppermost. |c| A diamond shape is formed where the edges meet. Cut a similar piece of coloured cotton fabric. Place the coloured fabric over the join and pin. |d| Turn the folded edges of the squares back over the coloured fabric. |e| Hem through all the layers.

Fabrics

It is much easier to work with soft, non-springy fabrics for the actual patchwork but any sort of fabric can be used for the coloured diamonds in the middle.

If you use a very dark fabric for the background and bits of silk and shiny fabrics

for the colours the patchwork will give the effect of windows at night. Alternatively, pale green hand-dyed calico with flowery patches will look like a flower garden. There are many interesting possibilities depending on the patterns and colours of the chosen fabrics.

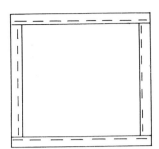

Cathedral window techniques.

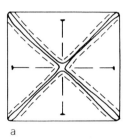

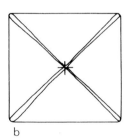

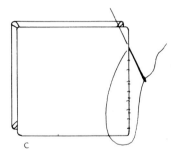

a   b   c

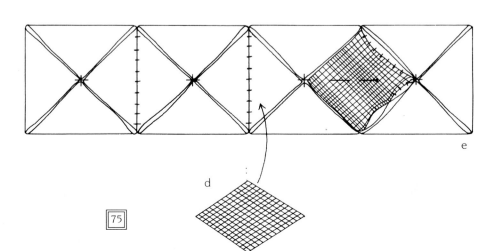

d   e

Left: Folded star mats and cathedral window napkin-holders. Sarah Mould, Julia Hall and Chloe Lawson.

75

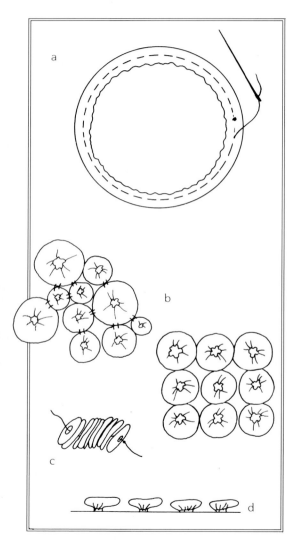

Gathered patchwork or Suffolk puffs

Method

|a| Cut circles of fabric about 4 cm (1½) in diameter. Turn in the edges and sew with running stitch, starting with a knot. |b| Pull the thread tight to gather up the fabric. Finish off securely and press flat. Join the little circles to each other at the edge with two or three stitches. |c| Alternatively, thread the gathered circles through the centre as if they were beads. |d| Turn the shapes upside down and sew to a background to create a knobbly texture.

Fabrics

Any woven fabric is suitable, and you can also include crochet circles. The circles can be large or small. Suffolk puffs look intriguing when you use see-through fabrics for the circles with scraps of other fabric pushed inside before you pull the running stitch tight.

Right: Boxes decorated with Suffolk puffs. Emma Lewis, Lucy Rainsford, Sarah Mould. Embroidered patchwork bedspread by Tracy Spencer.
Below: Caterpillars made from Suffolk puffs. Mary-Lou Witherington, Polly Harding, Carolyn Rools, Kate Halliwell.

Making up patchwork

owever beautiful or interesting a piece of patchwork, it will look much better if it is mounted or made up. Patchwork can be made up into various things, or can be used to decorate something else. Whatever you want to make, work out the design first, using paper and sticky tape, to make sure it will work.

Christmas tree decorations using a variety of patchwork techniques. Winchester Young Textile Group 1.

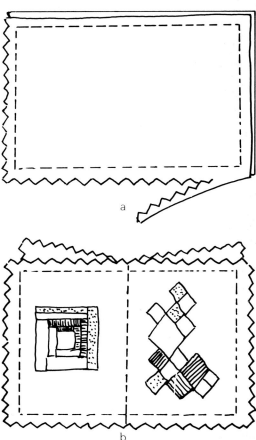

a

b

Making a rag book.

Pictures

Sew items of patchwork to a piece of matching fabric and stick on card. Blank greetings cards with ready-cut mounts are ideal for small pieces of patchwork.

Samples of small clusters of patchwork also look good when sewn on to calico squares and made into a rag book. Keep as a record of patchwork designs you have tried.

Put the patchwork itself and your designs for it between glass and hardboard and clip together to make a picture. Arrange them carefully in the frame – you might first cover the hardboard with a piece of patterned paper or fabric in a matching colour.

Make a picture composed entirely of borders both in patchwork and drawn on paper and frame it. The glass should hold the bits in position but it may help to put a scrap of double-sided sticky tape at the back of each piece.

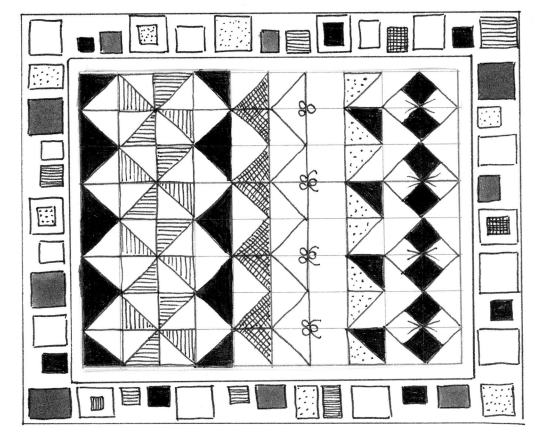

Making a picture from border patterns. The outside border is a collage of geometric shapes.

Wall hangings, banners and quilts

Wall hangings, banners and quilts are made in almost exactly the same way. Many people enjoy working on large projects such as these with their friends or with colleagues. This might be to mark a special occasion, to hang in a meeting place, or to make money for charity. People have been getting together to create this sort of community patchwork for many years.

Patchwork is ideal because each person can work on one small piece, the blocks being joined together afterwards. A patchwork of blocks of pattern made all by one person can of course be assembled in the same way. You will probably find it easiest to do this on the floor unless you have a very large table.

Working as a group

Colours, materials, method and pattern should be worked out before the project is begun. When a group is working together

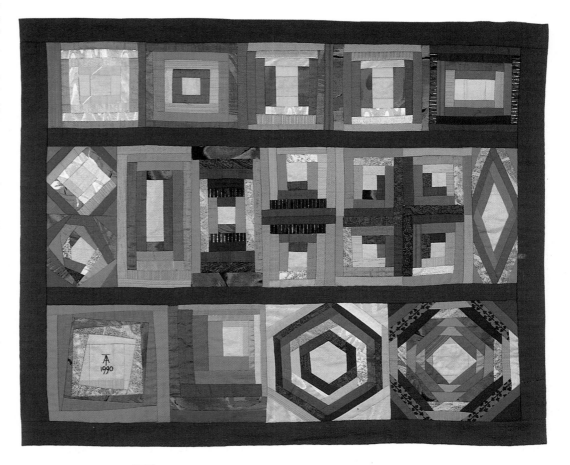

Sampler hanging: various ways of piecing a log cabin block. Note the subtle tones of colour achieved by using a variety of fabrics of different fibres (see p.47). Alice Timmins.

these points should be discussed and agreed by everyone.

Decide on the exact size and position of each piece. Remember to include seam allowances. It is essential that each shape is simple and that all the shapes interlock. Squares, rectangles or hexagons, or irregular but interlocking shapes can all be used.

Draw out the design, photocopy it, and give each person a copy of their own part. Everyone involved should have a written brief with clear details of what they are going to do and how.

Assemble all the materials and check that everyone has enough for their section. It is a good idea for the group to meet at regular intervals to make sure all is going well.

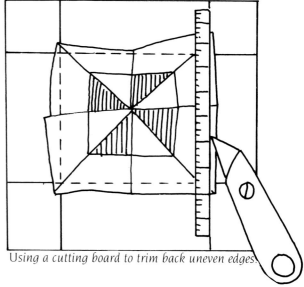

Using a cutting board to trim back uneven edges.

When the individual pieces are finished they can be machined together. Problems can sometimes occur when several people are each making a block. Usually this is because:

a] one of the blocks is too small to fit, in which case you add strips of fabric to all the edges (as in log cabin);

b] one of the blocks has uneven edges or inaccurate angles. If this is so, draw the correct shape on a larger sheet of paper,

Banner: embroidered patchwork squares. Sheffield Young Textile Group.

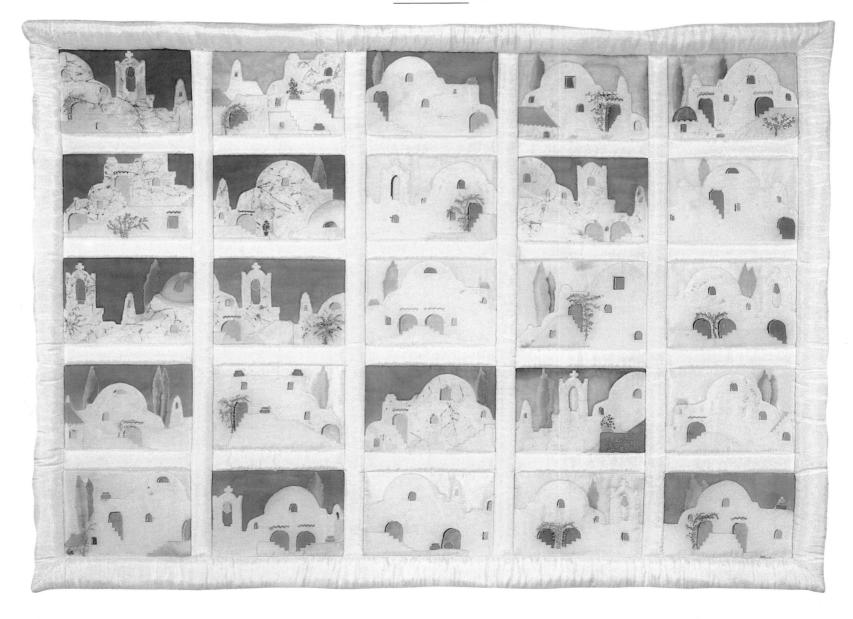

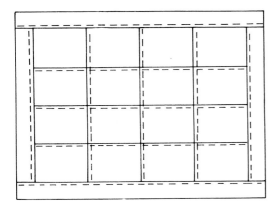

Lines of quilting.

extending the lines to the edge. Place the work on this and, with a ruler and fabric marker, mark out the shape, using the lines on the paper as guidelines, then cut the piece to size. Alternatively, you can use a cutting board and rotary cutter.

Finishing off

It is a good idea to line hangings and banners with another piece of fabric to give a neat finish. For body and warmth quilts are usually interlined with wadding as well. Again, work on a big table or on the floor to keep everything flat.

Left: 'Shades of Greece' by Caroline Harland. Patchwork hanging of silk painted rectangles.

Method without wadding

Cut a piece of firm woven fabric the same size as the patchwork – cut on the straight grain of the fabric. Pin, then tack, with the right side of the patchwork facing the right side of the lining. Machine all round the edge, leaving a gap at one side to turn the work inside out. When you have done this, stitch up the gap.

Quilting: The quilting stitches will hold the patchwork and the lining together. Spread the lined patchwork on a table and pull it into shape so that the lining and the top are flat. Tack right through both layers so they hold together firmly. Using smooth thread, work a running stitch along the lines between the pieces, going through both top and bottom fabrics. Alternatively, machine with straight stitch.

Hanging

This can be done in different ways (see diagrams).
a] Sew curtain rings or loops along the top at the back of the wall-hanging. Hang on a pole.
b] Sew a tube along the top at the back. The fabric you use should be firm, woven and cut along the straight grain of the fabric. Make sure it is wide enough to slide through a dowel or wooden pole. This is a very good method of exhibiting a quilt as the weight of the materials is supported evenly.
c] Sew velcro along the top edge. Staple the other piece of velcro to a strip of wood screwed into the wall.

If you are working alone, you might want to make a hanging but feel it would take too long. Sew small pieces of patchwork to larger squares or rectangles of contrasting fabric, perhaps a fabric you have dyed or printed yourself. Join the pieces.

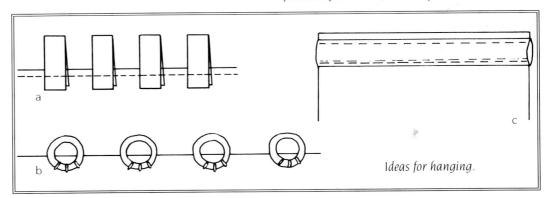

Ideas for hanging.

Alternatively, add several borders as if you were doing a log cabin on a larger scale (see p.44). These borders might also be printed with a pattern to link with the patchwork. Line and quilt as above, and add hanger/s.

Method with wadding – making a patchwork quilt

Patchwork is ideal for making a bedquilt, a throw or a cot cover. Assemble the patches in units as described above and join together, or separate them with strips first.

Work out the colours and tones, pattern and size of the quilt before you begin; ideally, you should also have collected the

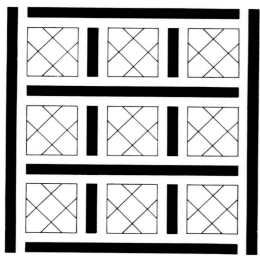

Assembling patches and boarders to make a quilt.

'Venetian pavements' quilt: dyed cotton, printed and coloured using a variety of techniques (detail p.41).

fabrics together, too. Often, a patchwork quilt can be designed so that it is made in sections, which are then joined up. A border or several borders can also be added.

Use a mixture of hand and machine stitches to make the top and quilt by machine or by hand.

Wadding

In the past, quilts were made of the unworn parts of old clothes and interlined with worn blankets. Today, people usually interline their quilts with wadding. This is an insulating material, often made of terylene, but sometimes of wool, cotton or silk. You must decide which material best suits what you are making but many fabric shops, department stores and craft suppliers stock rolls of wadding and most are pleased to advise.

Wadding is sold in various weights and widths, the most generally available weights being 2 oz or 4 oz, and either is suitable for a quilt. You need a piece of wadding the same size as the quilt top. If you have to join it, it should be abutted and not over-lapped.

Lay the quilt top right side to the floor, or on to a table, making sure there are no

The Blossom quilt designed by Peggy Pounce, made in blocks by quilters in the Wessex area and made up by Bristol Quilters (details pp.3, 57, 63 and 65).

creases. If you cannot do this from lack of space, work on one area at a time, taking great care to keep the whole as straight as possible.

Place the wadding on the top. Starting in the middle where possible, pin and tack the wadding to the quilt top.

Lining

The lining should match the quilt top in colour and type of fabric. Cut it to the same size at the top.

Place the lining on the wadding, making sure all three materials are straight and flat. Pin and tack through all three layers, starting from the middle and working towards the edges. Do plenty of tacking because this holds everything together. Lines of tacking every 10-15 cm (4-6in) both horizontally and vertically are not too much.

Quilting

The quilting stitches hold everything together and also make the lovely, indented patterns. The quilting patterns should link in with the design of the whole quilt.

Quilting can be worked on a quilting frame, which holds the whole quilt in position, or done in sections, using a large quilting hoop or embroidery frame.

Quilt: log cabin patchwork using matching furnishing fabric as a centre square. Rose Thomas.

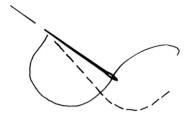

Quilting stitch.

Quilting by hand: Work the quilting stitches round the shapes on the quilt or draw out a pattern and quilt along this. There should be enough stitches to hold the three layers together securely, and they should be distributed evenly over the whole surface of the quilt.

Use a sharp needle and quilting cotton, machine embroidery cotton (no.30), fine coton-à-broder or buttonhole silk. Any smooth thread which will pass easily through all the layers is suitable. You can use different threads in different sections if you want. The stitches should not be too small or they will pull through the fabrics. Make stitches which are big enough to see and make a pattern.

Start with a knot. Ideally, this should be pulled through to be caught in the wadding, but that is not always easy. Just make sure of a firm start and finish off firmly, too.

Quilting by machine: Some machines have a quilting foot. However, if you just slightly loosen the tension on the general purpose foot, this should be enough to stop the three fabrics from dragging. Roll the quilt tightly from the edge so that it will fit under the machine comfortably. Hold it in place with cycle clips.

Start quilting across the middle using a medium length stitch.

The edges

Cut separate strips of fabric to bind the edge. These can be cut on the cross or as a straight strip.

Purses, bags and other small items

A rectangle of patchwork can be made into a simple bag or purse. Just to make sure that the bag is the right shape and size, work out a paper pattern of the design you want to use. Pin or tape this together. Line the patchwork with a piece of matching woven fabric in the same way as you might line a hanging, leaving a space to turn it right side out. Alternatively you can also use a layer of wadding and quilt the patchwork before making up.

Fold the patchwork rectangle either in two, or in three to make a flap. Oversew the seams, or add a gusset and oversew.

To make a handle take a strip of fabric cut on the straight grain. Fold down the length. Machine across the end and down the side. Turn inside out. Turn in the open end and oversew. Press.

Small objects like pincushions, needlecases and toys can all be made with just a few patchwork pieces arranged in the right way.

Log cabin patchwork by Mary Sumpter, patchwork clown by Sarah Williams, square patchwork bag and fabric background printed with transfer crayons by East Sussex Young Textile Group.

For a pretty Christmas decoration oversew two patchwork shapes together, with a piece of card between, then decorate with glittery beads and sequins.

Strip patchwork: bag by Amy Lampard, nightdress case by Heather O'Malley.

Cushions

S mall pieces of patchwork can be used to make cushions. Make or buy an inner cushion pad.

Top: Make the cushion top with a piece of patchwork, or a small piece of patchwork with borders, or a small piece of patchwork sewn on to a larger piece of matching fabric. It should be about 6mm (1/4in) larger all round than your cushion pad.

Back: Cut a matching piece of fabric for the back. This should be wider than the top to allow for the opening as well as the side seams. Cut this piece in half, turn in the edges and sew in a zip, or overlap the two sides and tack.

Place the two pieces right sides together and sew all round the edge. Turn out through the zip or the opening.

Somerset patchwork cushions. Sally Peters and Rosalind Massey.

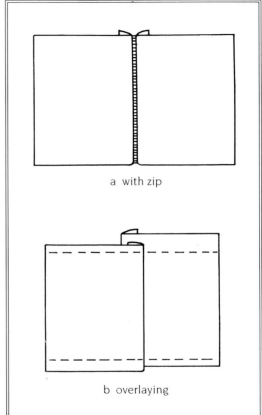

a with zip

b overlaying

Above: Making a cushion back.

Nine square patchwork cushions. Dawn Finney, Helen Lewis, Lucy Rainsford, Theo Palmer. Rubik's cube by Elizabeth Tone.

CONCLUSION

In the past many people had no leisure time at all. In spite of this, by making patchwork, they managed to combine creating something beautiful with making something useful: things like bed covers, clothes and furnishings. They had the satisfaction of producing something attractive, personal and unique. Many people still feel that it is satisfying to make something they can use.

Others simply like the way fabric patches interlock and how different materials look together. They are not really interested in whether the whole thing might drop to pieces after a few months, or whether it will wear out. They use fabric as you might use paint, to make splashes of colour, or as you might use crayons and pencils to make patterns. They just like to express themselves in fabric instead of paint. After all, just having something beautiful to look at gives you a lot of pleasure.

It is interesting to try using patchwork in both ways. There is plenty of room for everyone to do what they want and produce unique and exciting pieces of work.

Patchwork has no age barrier and the photographs in this book show work done by people with ages ranging from five to eighty-five. If you are interested in meeting others who enjoy patchwork and other textiles, many community and adult education centres offer classes and courses. The Quilters' Guild, The Embroiderers' Guild and The Young Textile Group of the Embroiderers' Guild welcome new members. There is now a City and Guilds module in patchwork and quilting. So – start now!

Silk patchwork purses. East Sussex Young Textile Group.

SUPPLIERS AND FURTHER READING

Suppliers: Materials and fabrics for patchwork, fabric paints and dyes, etc, are readily available in the haberdashery department of many large stores such as The John Lewis Partnership.

Textile craft suppliers, including patchwork fabrics and supplies are listed in Yellow Pages or white pages in the USA. Many of these smaller shops are happy to advise.

Mail order firms: Schools and Groups: NES Arnold, Ludlow Hill Road, West Bridgford, Nottingham NG2 6HD; C.W.Edding (UK) Ltd, Merlin Centre, Acrewood Way, St Albans, Herts, AL4 0JY.

Individual suppliers are advertised in specialist magazines such as *Embroidery Magazine*, PO Box 42, East Molesey, Surrey KT8 9AU; *Needlecraft*, Future Publications, Beauford Court, 30 Monmouth Street, Bath BA12AX; *The Quilter* (Quilters' Guild Magazine), 56 Wilcoy Road, Pewsey, Wilts SN9 5EC.

Further reading:

Sheila Betterton, *Quilts and Coverlets from the American Museum in Britain*, American Museum in Britain, 1978

Jenny Bullen, *Patchwork: From Beginner to Expert*, Batsford 1992

Valerie Campbell-Harding, *Fabric Painting for Embroidery*, Batsford, 1991

Valerie Campbell-Harding, *Strip Patchwork*, Batsford, 1989

Averil Colby, *Patchwork*, Batsford, 1987

Averil Colby, *Patchwork Quilts*, Batsford, 1988

Anne Coleman, *Collage, Appliqué and Patchwork: A Practical Guide*, Bishopgate Press 1992

Anne Coleman, *Quilting: New Dimensions*, Batsford, 1991

Robert Field, *Geometric Patterns from Roman Mosaics*, Tarquin Publications 1988

Anita Hallock, *Fast Patch*, Chilton 1992

Anne Hulbert, *Machine Quilting and Padded Work*, Batsford 1992

Jill Kennedy and Jane Varrall, *Silk Painting: Techniques and Ideas*, Batsford, 1991

Jan Messent, *Design Sources for Patterns*, Crochet Design, 1992

Jan Messent, *Design with Pattern*, Crochet Design, 1992

Michele Walker, *The Passionate Quilter*, Ebury Press, 1990

INDEX